Little Family, Big Values

LESSONS *in* LOVE, RESPECT, *and* UNDERSTANDING *for* FAMILIES *of* ANY SIZE

The Roloff Family
with Tracy Sumner

A Fireside Book
Published by Simon & Schuster
New York London Toronto Sydney

Fireside
A Division of Simon & Schuster, Inc.
1230 Avenue of the Americas
New York, NY 10020

First Fireside hardcover edition April 2007

FIRESIDE and colophon are registered trademarks of Simon & Schuster, Inc.

Designed by Mary Austin Speaker

Manufactured in the United States of America

10 9 8 7 6 5 4 3 2 1

Library of Congress Cataloging-in-Publication Data
Roloff, Matt.
      Little family, big values / The Roloff family with Tracy Sumner.
            p. cm.
      1. Family. 2. Values. 3. Conduct of life. 4. Dwarfs—Family relationships. I. Sumner, Tracy. II. Title.
      HQ734.R715 2007
      306.87087'50973—dc22   2007001228

For information about special discounts for bulk purchases, please contact Simon & Schuster Special Sales at 1-800-456-6798 or business@simonandschuster.com.

ISBN-13: 978-1-4165-4910-9

ISBN-10:   1-4165-4910-2

To Joshua David Roloff (1964–1999)
A great son, brother, uncle, and friend who was with us
in this life for far too short a time. We all miss you and
think of you every day, and we look forward to being
reunited with you one day in the presence of our Lord.

Contents

Little Family, Big Values

Introduction

The Meaning of "Roloff Family Values"

IF YOU WERE TO travel west out of Portland, Oregon, and through some beautiful, gently rolling hills, you might find yourself on a thirty-four-acre farm called Roloff Farms.

That is our home and the home of our four children as well as an assortment of animals we keep as pets or livestock. It's also the site of a complete three-quarters-scale western town, a pirate ship on a pond, a three-story tree house, an almost full-sized medieval castle, a big pumpkin patch, one of the biggest zip lines in North America, and other projects we've either completed or have on the drawing board.

If you've had a chance to see the Learning Channel's "reality" television show *Little People, Big World*, then you have at least a little bit of a picture of what the farm looks like—and what *we*, the family living on it, look like too. You know that my wife, Amy, and I are little people—more commonly referred to as individuals with dwarfism—living

1

a busy life of work, running our home and farm, and most important, raising our children.

One of the many results of doing the show is that we receive literally thousands of viewer e-mails every week asking us everything from what it's like to be small in a tall world to what kind of reactions we get from people when they first see us. But the question we're asked most often is what makes our family tick, how our mutual love, respect, and understanding have brought us beyond our differences to form a powerful family bond.

Those values are what this book is all about.

Our family—as varied as it is—works so well because Amy and I have had instilled in us by loving parents on both sides a set of family values, which we've built on and in turn instilled in our own kids. As a result, we now have our own set of family values, which we'll get into. Before we launch into our individual and collective beliefs, I'd like to introduce myself and my family for those who haven't come to know us through the show *Little People, Big World.*

The Story of Our Family

I was born a diastrophic dwarf, meaning that I am not only short in height—just over four feet—but I also have severe problems in my legs, knees, hips, shoulders, arms, and the rest of my body. My joints, my hands, and my feet are all visibly deformed. The list goes on and on.

All these physical problems led to a childhood spent in hospitals, either receiving corrective surgeries (some of which helped, some of which didn't) or recovering from them. In addition to those hospital stays (nearly two years combined), I spent more months than my family can count at home in braces and casts and recovering from my many surgeries. The physical problems have also led to a situation where it is impossible for me to stand up straight or walk without the aid of crutches.

Amy is also a little person, but her condition is different from mine and not nearly as severe. Her genetic condition is known in medical terms as achondroplasia, which is another cause of dwarfism but one that doesn't carry with it nearly as many of the complications as I've dealt with all my life. For the most part, Amy physically leads a fairly normal life in which she is active and even coaches our son's youth soccer team. For several years, she held the difficult but rewarding job of being a stay-at-home mom. However, in the past few years she has started working outside the home—part-time for a local youth soccer club and also as a preschool teacher.

We have been married for nineteen years, and we are the proud, happy parents of four children, the oldest of which are our twin boys, Zachary and Jeremy, who were born in 1990. We also have a daughter named Molly, who was born in 1993, and another son named Jacob, who was born in 1996.

Now, we know the question most people who don't know us would ask, and the answer is "No, not all of our children have dwarfism." While dwarfism of all kinds is a genetic condition that can and does run in families (for example, my brother Sam is also a little person), little people are very often the parents of average-sized children, and we have three of our own.

Our son Zachary, who is two feet shorter than his

twin brother, Jeremy, is the third little person in our family, making it a 3–3 tie between little people and average-sized people in our home. Zach's condition is the same as Amy's, meaning that he is relatively healthy.

The other two members of our family appearing on the show are my parents, Ron and Peggy Roloff, who have also contributed some of their thoughts to this book. As you will see as you read on, my parents are remarkable people.

My father is a tough but tender ex-Marine who instilled in me many of the values we've listed in this book. He is a man of incredible compassion, strength, and faith who knows what he believes in and why he believes it. He is also the perfect complement to Mom, who came from a background of comfort and ease only to take on the incredibly difficult job of raising four children, three of whom during certain points in their young lives required almost constant care and attention. Mom is a sweet but strong woman who could offer an encouraging smile while at the same time offering challenging words for children who needed to be strong to endure the pain of many major surgeries and countless hours of excruciating recovery and rehabilitation.

We are the Roloffs, and what follow are the values that make our family—which we admit is completely different from anything you've ever seen—what it is today.

Defining "Family Values"

Right from the start, there are some things we want you to know about us—namely things we *don't* claim to know or to be.

First, we are not counselors or experts who have this whole family values thing figured out. While we believe that the values you will read about in this book are all positive and helpful when it comes to family life, we don't by any means believe we have all the answers. In fact, sometimes we find ourselves drifting from those things we consider our most important family values. Like most families, we are learning and adjusting as we move along in life.

Second, though we have a happy, loving family in which our children are so far growing up to be well-balanced people, we aren't perfect by any definition of the word. As husband and wife and as parents, Amy and I have our share of conflicts, disagreements, and arguments. And our children, as much as we love them and would do anything for their well-being, aren't without their flaws either. At times, they argue with one another and demonstrate attitudes and actions that aren't as loving and supportive to one another as we would like.

In other words, we are, in most ways, just like any other family. Where we differ from other families with our physical challenges has given us more tests of our love and endurance than many, but that has served only to draw us closer to each other than ever. So underneath the surface challenges to our family lies a tremendous amount of love and support for one another. While there are times when it might not seem as though certain members of the family *like* each other, there is never a moment when they don't have love for one another.

Our family values are those things that are collectively important to us when it comes to living a good life. They are the things that we as parents feel are important to teach, instill, and be examples of when it comes to raising our children. They are the things that we hope our children will take with them when they are grown up and moving away from home to go to college, start their own careers, get married, and have children of their own.

Amy and I agree on the values that are most important to us, the ones that are not negotiable in our home. For example, faith and love and hard work are all values Amy and I have near the top of our lists. That's the way it is, and the way it will always be in this home.

However, there are some values we hold as a couple—even ones we've listed in this book—that we might not see eye to eye on when it comes to where they fit in the order of importance. It's not that we don't see all these values as important, just that if we were each to do a "top-ten list" of values for our family, the order of those values wouldn't be the same.

Take for example the value of commitment. While Amy puts commitment at or near the top of her list, I would put it further down. It's not that I don't value commitment—I certainly do, especially when it comes to this family and our home. It's just that Amy tends to be more of a committed-to-a-fault kind of person, while I see most commitments—with some very notable exceptions—as flexible and negotiable.

We have found that having differences in our hierarchy of values actually creates a family atmosphere in which we complement each other, both as spouses and as parents. In other words, our little differences allow us to both feed off each other and make each other even better parents for our children. In fact, we have come to realize that if we had the exact same list of values in the exact same order, it is possible—even likely—that we as parents would be missing out on something when it came to teaching or guiding our children.

We think that family values are those deeply held standards that have been incorporated into your life through the influence of your own parents, siblings, and other family members. It's how you were brought up and what your own parents and other adults taught you. Sadly, there are too many children in our world today who grew up in a home with no values at all or a warped sense of values. That is one reason we believe it is more important than ever not just to preach or teach family values but to instill them in our children.

When we talk about our children learning the values we've listed in this book, I hesitate to say that they've been "taught" those things. We don't consciously sit down and discuss most of these things with our children. In fact, I'd say that it's not practical or even *possible* to approach family and life values that way. Instead, I would say that what Amy and I have done is *instill* those values in our children, and all from an early age.

There is a big difference between teaching a value and instilling it in someone. To instill means to inspire people, to implant something in them, to encourage them to adopt a value or way of thinking as their own. Instilling happens through the experiences of applying certain values and information and absorbing them into your very being. I liken it to wrapping someone in a value or belief system much as you would wrap your child in a blanket. Nothing makes a parent prouder than to see one of your children, in a real-life situation, spontaneously exhibit one of the values that you cherish as a couple. Amy and I have had that joy.

Despite having our differences when it comes to which values are most important, we do our best as parents to make sure that there is consistency between us—in other words, no contradicting one another when it comes to which values need emphasis in a certain situation or on a certain day.

I know that when I see Amy do the things necessary to instill a particular value in one of the kids—and sometimes that involves some parental discipline—it is important that she knows that she has my support. Likewise, it is important to me to know that Amy "has my back" when it comes to instilling these values.

One of the most important parts of instilling values in children is making sure we don't just talk about the values but also demonstrate them the best we can in every way we can. In other words, we try not to be do-as-I-say-not-as-I-do parents but parents who practice what they preach. One of the most important examples of this is our faith. Amy and I could talk about faith all we want, but if we don't demonstrate it in both the way we talk and the way we live, then it's just air coming out of our mouths.

And believe me, if we were like that, the kids would pick up on it, and the results would be far different from what we are enjoying now.

Family Values:
They're Not Just for Little People

I also believe that our disabilities have worked to our advantage in this area because they give such stark visual examples of how to put these values into practice. For example, when it comes to self-respect, our kids look at Amy and me and see that despite the fact that we are smaller than other people and, therefore, easier to overlook in some situations, we both have the kind of self-respect it takes to make sure that people know we're here.

Perseverance, another of the values we've listed in this book, is also easier to teach because in their father our children have grown up with a living, breathing example of someone who has had to learn the importance of persevering through sometimes extreme difficulties in order to enjoy success as a businessman, as a farm owner, as a husband, and as a father.

Although these values work well for us and fit in well with a family where both parents have physical limitations or differences, we believe they can apply to families of any size, height, or social class. And while we may place a higher value on perseverance—simply because I have had to persevere through so much more than most people—it is still a value that is important for every family to develop and instill.

Every individual and every family has its own strengths and weakness, triumphs and defeats, its own moments of tragedy and moments to celebrate. And it's the values you rely on in the midst of all those experiences that will go a long way in determining what kind of parents you are, what kind of family life you enjoy, and what kind of people your children turn out to be when they grow up.

As we've said, our family values and how we apply them is an ongoing process, and in many ways life in the Roloff family is by trial and error. But even when we mess up in applying these values—and we most certainly have and will continue to from time to time—we can always fall back on the strength we have in one another because of the foundation of love we have for one another.

One of the things we both hope and pray will happen—and believe will happen—when our children are all grown and starting families of their own is that they will look back on their time growing up in the Roloff family and think, "I was raised in a wonderful family, a family where Mom and Dad loved us and where they taught us all these values that have given us the opportunity to accomplish what we have and will accomplish and to have the kinds of families we have." And when our children have children, we hope our kids will dedicate themselves to instilling the values they learned from us in the grandkids, adding their own as they see fit. My greatest wish is to see our happiness reflected in the lives of our children and in their future children.

To us, that's the look of a successful and happy family—no matter how big or small, short or tall it may be!

—Matt

Roloff Family Value #1
Love One Another

Amy

ONE OF THE THINGS we hear about from fans of the television show is that I often seem exasperated, frustrated, or even angry at Matt. The cameras always seem to be on me right at the moment where I look like I am about to lose my temper with him. Of course, we get a flood of e-mails from viewers asking why I can't "cut my husband some slack" now and again.

That's good television, I suppose, and there is an element of truth to it. Yes, I get frustrated and angry at Matt sometimes. We're both imperfect human beings, and we have our share of conflicts and arguments. But make no mistake: there is a tremendous amount of love between Matt and me. We love each other and our children deeply, and our children love us and one another the same way.

That is why love is one of our most important family values.

Like many of the values in this book, love has many definitions and can be demonstrated in many ways. To start with, I believe it is good to learn to love yourself in a healthy, humble way. In fact, I go so far as to say that it's nearly impossible to love other people if you don't know how to love yourself.

There's an old saying that goes, "Love isn't love until you give it away." To me, that means your love has to be spoken verbally and demonstrated in the things you do. It means showing your love through words, through actions, through moments of affection. When you do those things, you remind your spouse and children just how much you love them and you give them a sense of security within the family. But how do we do that?

We start by accepting each other unconditionally and for who we are. We don't judge or condemn each other, and we don't hold on to grudges or allow our anger to divide us from each other or from our children.

When you love your spouse unconditionally and choose not to judge him or her and not to hold on to anger, you find that it's OK, even helpful at times, to have differences or arguments. That's because when the conflict is all finished, the love is still there. The same is true when it comes to how we love our kids. Like all children, ours need to be disciplined at times. But Matt and I both know how important it is, when the discipline part of being Mom and Dad is over, that we let our kids know that we still love them, think highly of them, and want the very best for them.

It's also important that our kids see that when Mom and Dad have an argument or difference of opinion about something—and no two people living together under the same roof for twenty-plus years will completely avoid having those kinds of conflicts—they still love each other just as much as before and are committed to working out their differences in a healthy way.

Matt and I have learned that in our family that love is kind of catchy. It's contagious in that when someone does something to demonstrate his or her love to another, it's only a matter of time before someone else does it too. We've found that to be especially true when it comes to displays of affection in our home.

Matt is much more open and demonstrative of his love than I am. He is more likely to express himself through touch and open displays of physical affection. I, on the other hand, like doing things for Matt to let him know that I love him and am thinking of him. For example, as Matt prepares to go away on a business trip, I like to place a card in his bag with a note telling him that I love him and look forward to his coming home. While Matt is not wired to express himself that way, he has his own ways of demonstrating his love, and they mean just as much to me as my leaving him a note or card in his bag means to him.

Matt and I know that the kids see the love we demonstrate to each other, and so our kids are all prone to expressing their love for us and for one another. They are all comfortable walking up and hugging Mom and Dad and telling us they love us.

Love is an important family value because as parents, Matt and I want our kids to never doubt that we'll always be there for them, that we'll always love them no matter how many mistakes or poor choices they make and no matter what kind of chaos they get themselves into. We want them to understand that even when we don't like the things they are doing, they can always count on our love to see them through.

SOMETIMES LOVE MEANS
STAYING PUT

Matt

When I was a kid, we moved around a lot. I can remember living in at least six different homes in California's San Francisco Bay area. Each move meant going to a new school, making new friends, and getting acquainted with new neighbors.

I don't know if I have some inborn sense of adventure, but to me that was a pretty good life. I not only never had a problem with moving, I kind of enjoyed it and found it exciting. Yes, there was a little anxiety, because when you move you have to start up at a new school and adjust and acclimate yourself to a new environment and even get used to living in a new home. There were also adjustments to make simply because I was a little person, and any kid who is in any way "different" knows how hard it can be to break in at a new school or neighborhood. You have to go through all the stares, pointing, and questions all over again.

For the most part, though, I enjoyed the changes moving brought when I was a kid, and I don't think they really did me any harm. I'd even go so far as to say that they equipped me with some of the skills I need as a salesman and speaker. Now I am more comfortable acclimating to something new and walking into a new environment and asserting myself with the people who are there. That's always helpful when you are a salesman!

My wife and I have lived on our farm for the better part of two decades. Each of our kids has lived here since they were born, so they've never known any other home or way of life. In that respect, their lives are the opposite of mine growing up. Their lives aren't necessarily better, but they are greatly different.

I have to admit that I am by nature still a little on the restless side. You might even say that I have a slight case of wanderlust. This farm keeps me entertained and busy, and I love it here. But at the same time, there is a part of me that would like to spend some time in some other places—maybe relocate to Colorado for a few years, then spend some time in Texas, then move to Idaho.

I just think it would be fun to explore new places and new ways of life, and it appeared for a while that this could be a reality in my life and the lives of my wife and children. A few years back, employment opportunities and a probable move to another state threatened us with the very real possibility that we might have to sell the farm. It was during that time that I realized just how important this farm is to my children.

I realized that this piece of land has become the center of their lives, their security, their *home*. I also realized that the very best I can provide for my wife and these four children at this point in their lives is the security of home.

Amy has always been an anchor for me in that area.

She is the one who brings me back to reality when I start thinking about uprooting the family. She has on a few occasions let me know that moving would not be the best for the family and for its stability. And while the salesman in me always wants to focus on the adventure of living in a new place and meeting new friends, my love for my kids—with a nudge from my wife—always brings me back to what is best for the kids and not just what is best for me.

Once our children are grown and on their own, who knows? Amy and I may set out and do some traveling and live in some different places. Don't tell her I said that! But for now, Roloff Farms will remain home to Jeremy, Zachary, Molly, and Jacob and their loving parents.

> *Matt says:*
> *Love means giving your loved ones a sense*
> *of stability and security.*

LOVE MEANS PUTTING OTHERS FIRST

Amy

Sometimes it is in doing what is necessary that you find out you have a special gift. That is what happened when we were experiencing some financial challenges and Matt and I decided that I needed to take a job in order for us to get by.

I took a job teaching at a local church preschool, and it wasn't long before I realized that I loved teaching. I seemed to have a good rapport with the children. They loved me and I loved being with them and helping them to learn some of the very basics they would need as they continued their educational lives. I found the experience of teaching them personally rewarding. I just got a charge out of seeing these little four-year-olds learn and grow before my very eyes. Soon, it wasn't about money—although we needed it at the time—but about doing something I enjoyed and found personally fulfilling.

As far as I was concerned, I had found something I loved doing and didn't want to stop doing it. I wanted that sense of productiveness and contribution I felt to continue, so I planned to continue working as a preschool teacher for as long as the school would have me.

It was about that time, though, that I realized I had a higher calling, one I had to devote myself more fully to following. It was the very serious and solemn calling—and I believe it is just that—of being the best mother I can be to my four children.

I started to notice some things in the kids, especially Jacob, our youngest son. I still spent time with him coaching his soccer team, helping him with his homework, and other "mom" things. And in many ways, he seemed to be doing just fine with the situation we were in. But I wasn't able to spend much one-on-one time with him, and I could see he was starting to develop a bit of an attitude and wanted to do things that weren't appropriate for his age.

On top of that, we found out that Zachary was going to need surgery, so he was going to need me to be home to take care of him while he was on the mend. From there, the list of my children's needs seemed only to grow before my eyes. It was time for me to make a decision.

By that time, Matt was working full-time at an even better job than he'd had before, and we didn't need the money anymore. Matt and I talked about it and came to the conclusion that we didn't financially need for me to be working anymore. And while I still loved teaching and didn't want to quit, I knew that it was time for me to put what I wanted on the back burner and rededicate myself to making being Mom my one and only job. That is exactly what I did, and it wasn't long before we started seeing the benefits, both in our marriage and in the lives of our children.

In the future, when my children are older and don't

need quite as much attention, I may pursue a career in education more seriously. It's not impossible that I may even go back to school myself to get the credentials I need to be a schoolteacher. But for now, I know that my children need me, and I'm not only sacrificing what I want for their sake, but I am doing it willingly and joyfully—just because I love my children so much.

For now, I don't have any real career plans other than being the very best mom I can be. And as personally rewarding and satisfying as teaching other people's children is, it is nothing when I compare it with being Mom to my own kids.

Amy says:
Truly loving others—especially your children—often means delaying or forgoing what you want and making sure your full attention is on them when they need you most. That is a love that sacrifices self for the benefit of those you care about most.

LOVE MEANS BEING THERE
FOR YOUR FAMILY

Zachary

In our family, surgery has become kind of routine. Dad has had more surgeries than I can count, and Mom has had a few. Even my youngest brother, Jacob, had surgery after he was hurt when he got clonked by the trebuchet, a catapult-like thing we were using to launch pumpkins. I've had seven surgeries to correct some of the problems in my body.

But one thing that never changes in our family is when someone has a surgery or anything like that, the rest of the family is there for them. Mom said that each and every surgery is its own important event, and because we love one another, we want to go above and beyond the love we show the rest of the time. That's because people in the family want to do what it takes to make sure that the others are cared for when someone is sick or hurt.

My most recent surgery was last Christmas. It was to correct some problems in my leg. As strange as it may sound to someone who hasn't had to go through the things my parents and I have, in order to fix my leg, the surgeons actually had to *break* it in three places—at the knee, the ankle, and the femur (that's the big bone that goes through your thigh)—and put wedges and metal plates in.

As you can imagine, the recovery was painful. I had to take lots of painkillers and I slept a lot. But what really helped me get through it was that my family was with me. Dad couldn't be in the hospital the whole time, but he spent a lot of money and went to a lot of trouble to make sure that I was as happy as I could be. Mom stayed with me the whole time; she even slept in my room just in case I needed something. My brothers and sister helped me out just by hanging out with me and getting me things I needed when I couldn't walk.

The whole family even stayed during the holidays, so I wouldn't have to miss school and soccer season or wear a cast during a hot summer. Mom said she wanted me to understand that even though Christmas break is a great time to unwind and celebrate the season, she knew that having the surgery was a much bigger bummer for me and that the family wanted to be here to support me and comfort me.

I'm glad my family was with me through it all. And I'm also glad that times and hospitals have changed so much since my dad was a kid. Back then they had visiting hours, so his family couldn't be with him as much as he wanted.

As it was, everyone was with me and that made the pain not as bad. And I know they did that because of the love we have in our family.

Zachary says:
Within a family, there are all kinds of
chances to show we love one another,
especially when someone's in the hospital.

LOVE MEANS SACRIFICING
YOURSELF

Jeremy

I love Christmas break. You don't have to go to school, you get to be with your family, and you get to go hang out with your friends and do fun things and not have to worry about homework or soccer practice or anything.

As much as I love Christmas break is how much I hate being in hospitals. When someone is in a hospital, it's because they are sick or hurt, and that's not fun to be around. And it's even less fun when you have to be in a hospital over Christmas break. But when my twin brother Zachary—or any other member of my family—is in the hospital, then too bad not wanting to be there.

Last Christmas, I was stuck in a hospital in Oakland, California, where Zachary had some surgery done on his right leg. It was a pretty big operation, and he was in a lot of pain afterwards. And while I wasn't in the hospital room with him the whole time he was there, I did spend a bunch of time visiting him and helping him.

Dad and I were scheduled to fly back to Portland on the Thursday night before Christmas, which was the Monday following the surgery. We were just about set to go, and I was looking forward to getting back to see my girlfriend and hang out with my friends, who were planning a trip to Mount Hood Meadows to do something I love: snowboarding.

After the surgery, Mom and Dad said Jeremy was going to recover just fine. My friends had called me and said new snow was falling and the slopes were rad. They just couldn't wait for me to get home so we could go up there and make a day of it.

But then, Dad hit me with a change of plans. Instead of flying back early, he was going to stay in Oakland and drive back home when Zach was able to travel. And oh, by the way, would I mind staying to help load all the junk in the car and do the driving?

Dad made it clear that the decision was up to me. He came to me and said, "You know, I'm going to stay, and I think it would be cool if you stayed. You can go back if you want, and nobody would be mad if you did. It's your choice."

At first, I didn't know what to do. I had a girlfriend back home who was calling and wondering when I'd be back, and my two best friends calling telling me to get my behind home so we could go play in the snow. On top of that, a good friend of mine who has been living in Utah was in town and wanted to get together to hang out. It seemed like my phone wasn't going to stop ringing unless I got on a plane for home.

Dad had said it was completely and totally my decision. Now I had to make up my mind what I was going to do.

I struggled at first, because I knew Zach wanted me to

stay. I also knew that those "small" chores that need to be done before you can take a road trip from Oakland to home would have been trouble for the rest of the family without me there to help out. I slowly saw that my family needed me there. My friends—as well as those beautiful slopes calling my name at Mount Hood Meadows—were going to have to wait.

I stayed in Oakland the few extra days, then helped pack the car, which meant loading the luggage rack, which no one in my family would have been able to do. Then I had to drive the whole family home.

I knew it was the right decision, and I'm glad now that Dad let me make it for myself.

Jeremy says:
When it comes to the people you love,
sometimes you have to put off or even
cancel the things that could otherwise keep
you from being where your family needs
you to be and doing what they need
you to do.

A PICTURE OF LOVE
IN ACTION

Peggy

The world gets to see a side of Amy Roloff that, while it is real, doesn't tell the whole story about her, about her devotion and willingness to drop everything for those she loves when they call on her for help.

Ron and I saw that for ourselves, up close and personal, as Amy extended her love and concern to us in a time when we needed her.

On a very rainy and windy Oregon night not too long ago, Ron was hurt when he totaled his minivan. It was a near head-on collision in which the air bags didn't deploy properly and the seat belts didn't catch until he had been thrown violently forward, breaking his sternum.

I wasn't with Ron at the time of the accident, but I was called almost immediately after the emergency crews arrived. I didn't have a car—at least one I could drive that night—to get to the hospital, and knowing nothing more than the fact that Ron had been injured and was in an ambulance, I was in a panic.

I had no idea what to do, so I opened my cell phone and saw Amy's name first. I pushed dial and just prayed that she was available to answer.

Thankful to hear her voice answering the phone, I said, "Amy, this is Mom. Ron has been in an accident. They say he's OK, but he is over at Saint Vincent's and I don't have a ride."

At that time, Amy had been busy with the TV show, busy with the kids in soccer, and busy just being Mom. She didn't have a moment to spare. But when I called her, I realized immediately that she was ready and willing to drop everything in front of her and come to my rescue. "I'll be there in ten minutes," Amy told me, then hung up the phone.

Amy darted over to my home and picked me up and took me to the hospital to see Ron. As we arrived at Saint Vincent's, I told her, "It's OK for you to just leave me off. I know you have a lot to take care of." But Amy wasn't having that. "No!" she said. "I'm staying with you," and she did, until 10:30 that night, when Ron was released to go home.

In Amy's mind, there was no way she was going to leave when one of her loved ones was being treated in a hospital and another was in the waiting room.

This story is an example of the kind of love there is in the Roloff home, and it's a part of what makes the Roloff family what it is today. Though Amy is a very busy woman, she is willing to do any act of kindness and service for someone she loves.

Peggy says:
Real love means being willing
to drop everything to help someone you love
who is in need, no matter how busy
you may be.

Roloff Family Value #2
Commitment

Amy

WHEN IT COMES TO having a good marriage and being good parents, love and commitment go hand in hand. It is commitment that provides stability and strength in a family setting, and commitment that keeps people from running away from their obligations when life gets tough or when they just feel like they'd like to try something else for a while.

When it comes to my personal core values, commitment is one of the very most important.

To me, commitment is what comes from within a person of high character that motivates that person to stick by his or her word and convictions no matter what the personal cost. Commitment means that you have decided in your heart and mind that you are in something—such as a marriage or family situation—for good, and nothing is going to take its place on your list of priorities. Commitment means that you can be counted on to keep your word and your promises and vows to others even when you don't feel like it, even when those you have committed yourself to don't seem to appreciate it.

Commitment provides a bridge between those times when you feel like doing the things you've said you'll do and the times when you don't. Even in the happiest marriages and family settings, there are seasons when we don't feel like doing the things we know our spouses and children need us to do. But it's that unbending sense of commitment that gets us through those "down" times and overrides any negative feelings until we can get to a point where we can be emotionally recalibrated, rejuvenated, and refilled.

If there is one thing Matt and our four children know beyond any shadow of doubt, it's that I love all of them deeply and that I am committed to them and will always be here, no matter what. I am not going to run away when things get difficult—or even when one of them gets difficult. And when I say I'm not going to run away, I don't mean just physically. I'm talking about emotionally and spiritually, meaning that I'll be there for them in body, mind, and spirit.

I know that when I'm upset with Matt or when the kids are acting up, there is a small part of me that wonders if it wouldn't be easier if I weren't in the family situation I'm in. But there is a bigger part of me (and I'm happy to tell you that it's *much* bigger) that makes me realize that no matter how much my husband or kids frustrate me (and they most certainly do), it is not nearly enough for me to let go of them either physically or emotionally, simply because of the commitment I have made to them.

Sadly, too many people in our culture today take their commitments too lightly. You can see that in the high divorce rates and in the lack of involvement of so many parents in their children's lives. It's as if they've taken an old saying and twisted it around: "When the going gets tough, the tough get going . . . right out the door."

Nineteen years ago, I stood before my God, my family, my friends, and Matt and made a series of vows. One of those vows contained the phrase "Till death do you part." That's commitment—a lifelong commitment. And it's one that has helped our family to grow together in love for all these years.

Making and keeping commitments requires some serious thought as well as a good sense of priorities. Though I take all my commitments very seriously, there are some that have crossed the "seriously" threshold and become *absolute*. For example, my commitment to God and to my marriage and my kids is absolute. After that, I have commitments to other family members, commitments to friends, and commitments to neighbors and even the kids on my soccer team. But while there are different levels of commitment, it is still important to keep them all as well as you possibly can.

One of the reasons I say that is because I know I have four sets of eyes watching me and, in their own way, scrutinizing me to see if I really do as I say and not just what is convenient or easy for me. Matt and I try to instill a strong sense of commitment in our children in every way we can. We want them to understand that when they give their word, they don't just back out without a good reason or without trying to find alternatives. We want them to know that when they make a commitment to something or to someone, they should do everything they possibly can to follow through on that commitment.

And most of all, we want them to know that, along with love, it is commitment that has provided for them a home in which they can feel secure and free to grow into adults.

COMMITMENT MEANS FINISHING
WHAT YOU START

Matt

One of the things Amy and I teach and try to demonstrate to our children is that commitments aren't something to be either made or broken in some willy-nilly fashion, that before they make a commitment, they need to think very carefully about what it's going to take to keep it and how long it's going to take. Likewise, we teach them that you don't break a commitment unless you have a legitimate reason for doing so. That is the part of commitment where Amy and I differ; I believe there is a time and a place to break certain commitments.

One recent example of that in my life occurred when I was president of the Little People of America (LPA), an organization dedicated to the rights and concerns of little people. I had lost my job following the September 11 attacks. There wasn't a lot going on in the high-tech sector of the economy, so I decided to take some time off and serve LPA, which I did as president.

Later on some business opportunities presented themselves to me, and I began thinking about resigning a bit early so that I could pursue them. I knew that doing so would be of financial benefit to my family, and we needed the money. I certainly wasn't making anything as president of LPA—which was a nonprofit—but serving as a complete volunteer.

I was torn at that time. I was approaching the end of my presidency, and some good things had been happening in LPA with me as president. I also felt a sense of loyalty to the LPA because Amy and I and our son Zachary had benefited so much from being members. In fact, it was at the 1986 LPA convention in Detroit that Amy and I first met.

It was difficult for me to consider walking away from the LPA presidency, but it was equally if not more difficult to think about turning down the business opportunities I had. Before I made my decision, I did the one thing I felt sure I needed to do: I talked to Amy.

We had three options, the first of which was for me to resign the LPA presidency and put my focus on the business opportunities. The second was for me to focus primarily on the business opportunities but remain LPA president. The third was to ignore all business opportunities and just focus on my position as LPA president and even run for a second term.

My wife told me that I had done a wonderful job as president of LPA. She also pointed out that I was nearing the end of my term and that it wouldn't do my reputation or the family's any good for me to walk away before the end. She said that I needed to finish my term and do it to the best of my ability. "While you are winding this down, still give it your best to finish out the year as you find someone else to run for the next term as president," she told me. "But you need to continue this and fulfill your commitment."

Finally, Amy assured me that the family could hang in there financially for a little bit longer while I finished my term. That is exactly what I did. But if Amy had felt that the financial pressure on the family was too great, this would be a case—in my view—where one commitment could be broken in order to keep a higher commitment to the family. Life isn't so simple that commitments don't get entangled with each other and you can find that keeping one causes you to break another. In this case, there was a narrow path that let me + both commitments.

As it turns out, one of the reasons I was so successful as president of LPA is that I was able to put in more time and devote myself to serving much more effectively than someone who was working full-time. I was able to put more of myself into the job, and because of that I was able to institute some positive changes in LPA and its structure.

In the end, I had honored my commitment to the LPA while maintaining my loyalty to my family—simply because I had involved Amy in my decision. Because of that, I was able to preserve my own reputation and the reputation of my family. I also demonstrated to the kids the value of keeping a commitment to an organization that had earned my loyalty.

Matt says:

Sometimes keeping commitments involves delaying benefits for yourself or those you love and having to take a longer road to a goal. After taking that slower path and completing your prior commitment, you may find that your goal is still reachable.

A COMMITMENT TO
MY TEAM

Jeremy

A few years ago, there was a sports news report on TV where Allen Iverson, who played at the time for the Philadelphia 76ers, ridiculed the idea that he needed to go to basketball practice. In his mind, his going to practice wasn't going to do anything to make him or his team better. Even I knew that what he said was bogus.

It's no secret that I love soccer. I love the game, but not the practices. I want our school, Faith Christian Bible, to be the best but there are plenty of times I find myself thinking like Allen Iverson.

That's because as much as I enjoy soccer, I don't especially enjoy soccer practice. Sometimes practice is fun, but most of the time we have to run through drills and things we've been doing all year. I know that my coach has us doing those things to shape up the team, but sometimes I just don't feel like spending my time doing them.

There have also been plenty of times when I didn't want to go to soccer practice simply because I wanted to go and do something else. One time when I wanted to go out and hang with my two best friends and my girlfriend, two things happened. First, Mom wouldn't call the coach for me and tell him that I couldn't go. "If you want to break that commitment and not go for that reason, you need to call him, not me," she told me.

It may sound like bragging, but I'm kind of a key player on the team. I started imagining how practice would go without me. I didn't have to be the coach to see it would throw off everybody else if I wasn't there. If we lost a game, how would I know it wasn't my fault for skipping practice?

One of the things Mom and Dad—Mom especially— always tell us kids is that if we go out for a sports team or whatever group we join, we need to keep our commitments to the team or group through the end of the season or the end of the year. That means going to all meetings and practices and doing the work it takes to be the best we can. Once the season is over, we are free not to come out the following year if we don't want to.

I'm glad my mom stepped in that day, and I've never forgotten my commitment to my team. It was important because it let people know they could count on me to do what I'd said I'd do when I first signed up, and I never want Coach or my teammates or my friends to think of me as a guy who doesn't keep his word.

Jeremy says:
Keeping commitments isn't always fun.
But when you keep your commitments,
people will see that you are a person
who can be counted on to do what you've
said you'll do, benefitting not just yourself
but all.

Roloff Family Value #3

Perseverance,
aka *Never Giving Up!*

Amy

WINSTON CHURCHILL, THE FAMOUS World War II–era British prime minister, gave his most famous—and shortest—speech at a college graduation ceremony, telling the soon-to-be graduates: "Never give up. Let me continue by saying: Never, never give up! And in conclusion I say to you: Never, never, never give up!"

Not only was that great advice, but it also defines one of the family values in the Roloff household: perseverance. And while none of us Roloffs have ever had to lead a nation through the darkest days of a terrible world war, we have had opportunity to learn what perseverance is all about as we've endured our own difficulties and challenges. Perseverance means that you keep going, even when things are difficult—*especially* when things are difficult. It means getting up every single day without asking, "Why me?" or saying, "I can't go on!" but instead saying, "What can I do to make today a great one, despite all that is going on in my life now?" and "Thank you, God, for thinking enough of me to allow me to have to endure the pain and difficulty I'm going through now." And it means knowing that there is a purpose in what you're enduring and making sure you keep your eyes open to find it.

Being little people, Matt and I have had more to persevere through than most people. We have had to deal daily with our physical limitations, Matt has had to go through surgeries and other painful medical procedures, and we've both had to take being "looked down on" because we are smaller and because we are "different."

However, this isn't all bad news. We have learned that there are, in a very real way, advantages in what we've gone through when it comes to learning to persevere through difficult times.

Now, most average-sized people might look at us and ask, "How in the world can you say there's an advantage to being little?" The answer to that is simple: When you are a little person in a big world—or when there is anything about you that makes you "different" to the point where people can't help but notice or that limits you in some area—that difference tends to make you stronger mentally and give you "muscles" of perseverance and resiliency that most people don't have because they've not had to endure any real difficulties—at least not on the level that we have.

Someone who has lived what looks like a "perfect" life—someone who is tall and handsome, with a perfectly healthy body that has never been sick one day, and who came from a loving family in which the parents are still together—will probably find the going a little tougher if something bad or difficult were to happen in his life. If everything is going well for someone like that, and suddenly he loses his job or his wife gets sick, then he's going to have a tough time and maybe spend a lot of his energy feeling sorry for himself.

In our family, however, we have the attitude that we don't have time to feel sorry for ourselves. Do we ever wish some of the situations we face could be different from what they are? Yes! Do we ever pray that God will give us relief from some difficulty we're enduring? Absolutely! But one thing we don't do is allow ourselves the luxury of self-pity. Instead we allow the difficulties to make us stronger.

Matt

One of life's simple truths is that bad things happen to good people (and the other way around, for that matter), and there have been things that have happened to me and to my family that I would rather have avoided. But I have come to a point of understanding that when life's negatives outweigh the positives, when things are going on around me that I just don't think are fair, that's an opportunity for me to build up my perseverance.

There is an old saying that goes, "Whatever doesn't kill you makes you stronger." I think that is why I'm where I am today. When I was a child, I went through many surgeries and countless hours of rehabilitation and other treatment, and even then God was using that suffering to make me stronger. Even back then, I never had a sense of "poor me!" and today I am reaping the benefits of persevering and overcoming that adversity.

Now when tough or negative things happen, I don't spend a lot of time moaning and crying about it. I'm able to absorb them and keep a positive attitude, knowing that because of what I've been through already, I'll have the strength to persevere and overcome whatever happens to me and to my family. If that means that Amy or I or one of the kids is sick and needs medical attention, we don't go into self-pity mode but just get it taken care of. If that means I lose a job I needed to support my family, I say, "It might be rough for a while, but something better is going to come along," then get out there looking for a new opportunity.

Perseverance is yet another value we have tried to instill in our children, and we do that by both encouraging and challenging them when they are going through difficult times at school or with their friends.

For example, there have been times when Zachary has struggled with the way kids treat him as a little person. We do give him some sympathy, but more important we give him a message very similar to the ones my parents gave me when I came home from school complaining and crying about the way the other kids treated me, and it's essentially this: "You've got to toughen up. You're not the only one to go through tough times, and it *will* get better."

In other words, *Never give up!*

PERSEVERING MEANS SEEING OPPORTUNITY IN ADVERSITY

Matt

Sometimes, you have to persevere through the consequences of what might at the time seem like a mistake in judgment. That is exactly what happened to me back in 2001, when I made what I thought was a great career move, only to have it blow up in my face.

I had worked for a software sales firm for about five years and had a great future with them. They were doing some great things, and I was a part of it. The company's potential as well as my own professional potential seemed almost unlimited.

I don't know if it was my sense of adventure, my wanderlust, my looking for the "bigger, better deal," or the fact that I am by nature something of a risk-taker, but I left that company—whose value by that time was in the billions—and took a job with a bigger company that offered me a better position and a higher salary.

Everything seemed in order for me to take off and grow in my new job—that is, until that horrible, historic event that has come to be known by two numbers: 9/11.

It wasn't long after the terrorist attacks of September 11, that the high-tech sector of the economy started taking a downturn. Before long, I and some of the other salespeople with the new company I had started working for were called to a business meeting on the East Coast. It was there that they announced some pretty massive layoffs. I was one of the casualties.

On the six-hour plane ride home, I went through an array of thoughts and emotions. I thought about how I could really let what had just happened get me down and keep me down, how I could just cry about it and worry and wonder about what was going to happen to me and my family next. I also remember wondering what I was thinking when I quit a great job to join a competitor that six months later kicked me to the curb.

I thought about those things, and I felt the negative feelings. But only for a moment!

As I sat there on that plane, I suddenly got hold of myself and stopped thinking about the negatives of what had just happened to me and started thinking about the opportunities that losing the "perfect" job offered me. I thought about some of the ideas I had been kicking around, about some of the business opportunities I had wanted to explore, about some of the ways I wanted to serve others as a member of Little People of America.

I started making a list of those things, and by the time I got off that long flight back home, I was free of any thoughts of self-pity or defeatism and completely energized and charged to go forward and make good things happen for me and my family.

I'm not going to say that the times since then have all been easy. Far from it! But our family has been coming back with a vengeance since the down times after September

11, and we continue to do so to this day. As of now, I am working full-time for a great company at a higher rate of pay than I got before, I've started my own company, and I'm starring in a television show. Not only that, I had the opportunity to serve a two-year term as president of LPA.

And all of that has happened because even in the face of disappointment and difficulty and setbacks, I refused to give up and instead moved upward and forward.

> *Matt says:*
> *Perseverance often means looking beyond*
> *what might seem like a dire situation*
> *so that you can have a plan to get through*
> *the tough times and even continue*
> *prospering through them. It often means*
> *getting up in the morning—no matter how*
> *tough the previous day was—putting on*
> *your boots (if you're a farmer like me), and*
> *looking forward to a new day.*
>
>

DOING WHAT PEOPLE SAY
YOU CAN'T DO

Zachary

One of the things any little person has to overcome is the fact that people automatically think you can't do certain things just because you're small. For me, that's been especially true when it comes to soccer.

I'm just like my twin brother Jeremy in that I love soccer. I like a lot of other sports, but soccer is my favorite. The difference between us is that Jeremy is tall and fast and that's part of being good at soccer. The game comes a lot easier for him, which is why he has such a key spot on our high school team.

But that doesn't mean I can't play the game, and it doesn't mean I'm about to give up.

Mom and Dad have been great about encouraging me to keep playing, even though there are a lot of players and coaches and parents who don't think I should be on the field. Average-sized players and coaches usually don't want to let me play because they look at me and see someone who's smaller or who can't run as fast because I have shorter legs. Or if they do let me play, it's only for a little bit—I guess so I can feel good about getting in a game.

When I went out for our high school team in my freshman year, I went to all the practices and worked hard and got better every day. But I wasn't getting in the games at all. Sometimes it's really hard for me to prove to people that I'm good. I've had to learn to be tough on the field because I'm playing against guys who are up to six feet tall, and a lot of the time I get banged around pretty good. But I've learned that if I'm going to prove myself and show that I can play soccer, I have to get right back up and get back at it.

Winter or summer, I'm trying to be a better soccer player. There are some days when it seems like I'm outside with a ball practicing from sunup to sundown—all because I really like to play soccer and want to be a part of my high school team. All that hard work paid off too, and because I didn't give up—and didn't quit bugging the coaches to let me play—I started getting on the field my sophomore year in high school.

Mom always says she worries because as much as I love soccer, it's harder for me to compete against taller players at the high school level. She has even tried to get me to take up some other interests, but it always comes back to soccer for me. And because I kept playing and didn't give up, I finally showed the coach and other players that I can do it.

I know that I will never be able to play soccer at the same level as my brother. That is why I think about being a coach, assistant coach, or referee. That way, I could stay involved in the game I love. I've already done some coaching with my mom and also taught some young people to play soccer. I like teaching, so that would be a double plus for me.

I study everything about soccer so that I can prove to people that I belong in the game. And I have learned that if I keep working hard and don't give up, I can prove to people that I can do things they say I can't.

Zachary says:
If you want to prove to people—even to yourself—that you can overcome things and succeed at something you love, you have to work long and hard and not let anyone's doubts get in your way.

PERSEVERANCE MEANS AVOIDING FUTURE REGRETS

Jeremy

I have a great time playing soccer, and I've done well as a forward striker. But nothing I saw in high school soccer—in practice or in the games—could have prepared me for what I saw at the Olympic Development Program (ODP) tryouts held after my freshman season. The ODP gets top kids from the whole state and puts them together with top coaches to help look for and develop Olympic contenders.

A lot of the players at ODP were from bigger schools, where there are more and better players to choose from. I am confident in my ability on the soccer field, but the first day of the ODP tryouts opened my eyes to just how good some of the players around the state of Oregon really are, especially the players from the bigger schools.

It was pretty overwhelming being on the same field as some of those players the first day of ODP, and to be honest, I didn't know if I wanted to come back for a second, I was so tired and sore. Some of those guys did things that just didn't seem possible for a high school player.

I talked to my mom about not going back, but she didn't want me to quit and wouldn't let me quit—not without giving me some things to think about. She told me, "Maybe this is a good lesson for you about how hard you need to work, even when things are easy." Besides, she said, being out there against those good players wasn't going to kill me. In fact, it might even make me a better player.

I thought about what Mom said and about Zach. He worked at soccer twice as hard as I did and would give anything he owned to get beat up on that field instead of me. If he wouldn't flinch at getting out there, why should I?

With Mom nudging me, I decided to go back to ODP for a second day, and I actually had a good day. I didn't score any goals, but I made some good moves and got off a few decent shots. I didn't think of myself as better than a lot of the players there that day, but I started to think that I could hang with them and give as good as I got. Not only that, I came out of that experience with more confidence in my game, that'll make me better next year.

Later, I realized that when I was talking to Mom about not going that second day, I was really looking for an out. But both Mom and Dad encouraged me not to give up just because things seemed rough on the soccer field. Looking back, I know that they would have let me if I'd really wanted to, but they weren't going to make it easy or let it happen without giving me something to think about first.

Jeremy says:
When you persevere and refuse to
give up even when you think you face
overwhelming odds, you won't end up with
regrets or wonder later on if you could
have accomplished more. You also just
might succeed.

PERSEVERANCE IS THE CAN-DO ATTITUDE

Peggy

Growing up, I was a very well-cared-for young woman who never had to do anything for herself. In hindsight, it's only by the grace of God that I have been able to endure the difficulties involved in raising three boys with severe physical limitations.

Though I am grateful to my mother and father for how they cared for me and nurtured me, it didn't take me long to realize that my boys just weren't going to make it in this world if they didn't develop perseverance. In the beginning they would have been lucky to be able to fight their way out of a wet paper bag when things got tough. For that reason, I allowed them—even *encouraged* them—to do for themselves as much as they possibly could.

I remember when Matt was about twelve years old. He wanted to buy himself a pair of skis, so he was going to have to earn himself some money, because Ron and I weren't going to just buy them for him. Matt's plan to earn the money was to take a newspaper route.

I never told Matt that he couldn't do it, and I wouldn't have. But at the same time, I thought to myself that he wasn't thinking this through, that there was no way he could do a paper route. For one thing, it would be hard for him to travel the distances it took to do the route, and for another, he couldn't even carry the bag high enough to keep it out of the grass.

When Matt told me he wanted to do the route, I told him to find out when and where he had to go to apply and I would drive him there. He did some research and found a twice-weekly paper in our area that needed delivery boys. I drove him to where they were taking applications, and there was a line of kids a half a block long. Matt got in line—wearing braces and crutches and standing belt-buckle high to the rest of the kids—and waited to see the manager.

As I waited in the car, I wondered how the manager was ever going to justify giving Matt a job. But as I waited, I saw Matt moving toward the car with a smile on his face. "I got the job!" he excitedly told me, then explained that the delivery route was the businesses right around the corner from us.

Matt showed amazing perseverance and determination just to get that job. But his perseverance continued and even intensified once he started the actual work. He had to get up at six every morning and fold the papers. When they were folded, he'd load them into our Volkswagen van. Then I would drive the route while he sat and threw the papers from inside the car. When a paper needed to be carried away from the street to be delivered, I stopped and let Matt do it.

Matt's grandmother scolded me and said that I should have been helping Matt more, but I told her, "No, that's his job, and I'm not going to do it for him." I didn't want to get in the way of Matt learning to do for himself and to keep at something even though it was difficult or took special effort.

Matt had to learn to persevere and to finish what he had started on his own. I knew that in allowing him to struggle on his own and get through difficulties without my help, I was setting him up to persevere later in life—when Mom and Dad wouldn't be there to help him out when he failed or pick him up when he fell.

> *Peggy says:*
> *Teaching and learning perseverance some-times means pushing ourselves or allowing ourselves to go beyond what might seem possible at a given moment, focusing not on the immediate obstacles but instead on the benefits of long-term success.*
>
>

Roloff Family Value #4
Respect—for Yourself
and for Others

Matt

IN THE ROLOFF HOME, we have done everything we can to teach and instill in our children, and in one another, the family value of respect—respect for ourselves as individuals and for everyone else.

In a very strange but very *real* way, we have made

respect an important value in our family because we've had to work so hard to earn it. We're not saying this to complain, but there is a tendency on the part of people not to respect little people, and that has meant that Amy and I have had to go the extra mile when it comes to earning and keeping the respect of those around us.

For example, if two little people—or people with any other kind of disability—were to walk into a car dealership at the same time as two tall people, the automatic response from the managers or salespeople is to assume that the tall person is more deserving of their time. It's almost as if they assume that the tall person has a higher position in his business, makes more money, and therefore is more likely to buy a new car. It's only when these two little people make themselves more visible to the salespeople and show that they are serious about buying a car that they are taken seriously.

About now, you may be thinking, *That's not fair!* And you're right! There's nothing fair or right about it, but it's our world and our reality, and we've learned that it's up to us to take our situations, learn from them, and make the very best of them as we work to earn the respect of people around us.

And it's also up to us to make sure that neither we nor our children use any disrespect against us—real or perceived—as an excuse to treat others disrespectfully.

Just as there are several kinds of love, there are also several kinds of respect. The first is simple respect for other people because as human beings they are God's special creations. Then there is the respect you give to people because of their position—your parents, your boss, your government and spiritual leaders. There is also the kind of respect you give to people because they've earned it, because you recognize something admirable and worthy of respect in them.

All of these kinds of respect are valid and important, and we do our best to instill them as a value in our children. We do that by teaching them and showing them that no matter how "different" someone is from them and how much they might disagree with someone's opinions, beliefs, or even actions—other than those that are patently objectionable, offensive, or sinful—they need to show that person a degree of respect. Yes, it's OK to disagree, even strenuously, with what someone is doing or how they talk or think, but it is never OK to treat that person disrespectfully.

In so many ways, showing respect to others has become a lost art. It wasn't that long ago that giving someone simple respect was a given, something people just did because it was the right and decent thing to do. Now so many people are so into self—self-enhancement, self-improvement, self-image, self-esteem—that they have forgotten how to treat others respectfully.

I see respect as a pendulum swinging from scoundrel to saint. We start at rest, at zero or basic respect for all. A person's words and actions move the pendulum in one direction or the other depending on his values and how he applies them. The basic technique for keeping your pendulum on a positive swing is to think before speaking and to pause before judging.

It's safe to say that most children at some time or

another give their parents the opportunity to correct them and teach them something about treating others with respect. I can remember a few occasions when we saw a homeless person or drove by someone standing on a freeway on-ramp holding a sign asking for money. Being kids, they made some sly comments to the effect that the person needed to get some self-respect, find a job, and stop bothering people by begging for money.

While I value hard work, dignity, and self-discipline, I also have come to understand that until I walk in someone else's shoes, I have no right to judge their intentions, their motivations, or their situations. I learned that at a young age because my father, who is as compassionate and as caring a man as I've ever known, very often brought home complete strangers—people who were what too many of us consider outcasts—and welcomed them to sit down at our dinner table to eat a warm meal with the family. What I learned from my father and have never forgotten is that everybody— whether rich or poor, dressed in an expensive business suit or wearing rags, the president of Nike or a cashier at the local convenience store—deserves basic respect.

That is a lesson I have tried to communicate to my kids when I point out to them that they don't know a person's circumstances and that they have no idea what he or she has been through or what brought this individual to this point. I tell them that they need to make sure they don't judge people by personal appearance or by what they are doing to get by in life. I try to teach my kids to show that person the respect he or she deserves as a human being who was created by God.

To me, that is where respect for others starts. It means looking at that person in his or her circumstances and honestly asking, "If I were where this person is now, if I were walking in his or her shoes this very day, how would I want to be treated?"

It means, as one great Man once taught, doing to others what you would want them to do to you.

It's a great value to live by, and that's why it's a value in the Roloff home.

MUTUAL RESPECT—
EVERYBODY WINS

Amy

You know by now that the Roloff family has a passion for soccer. Jeremy and Zachary both play on their high school varsity team and have played at several different levels. Our daughter, Molly, and our youngest son, Jacob, also play and just might follow in their big brothers' footsteps.

I love the game too. And though I was never able to play myself, I have become a part of the game and a part of my children's lives at the same time by taking up coaching. There is nothing I love better about being a mom than getting involved in my children's activities, and coaching looked like a great way to be a part of yet another aspect of their lives.

I've gone through six years of soccer with our older boys—from the kindergarten level up to high school—and I've picked up some great experience along the way. Also, I've interacted with parents and coaches, watched the game, and even attended some coaching clinics. I've learned enough about the game and about coaching it to be able to do what I think—and what others say—is a respectable job of coaching at the youth level.

Matt and the kids know that I have a tendency to be very

competitive, but they also know that my competitiveness is exceeded by my desire that, win or lose, the kids do their very best on the soccer field. Yes, I want the teams I coach to win. But it is more important to me how the kids represent themselves in their effort, their sportsmanship, and their character on the field. I respect the abilities of my team, not to produce wins but to show sportsmanship and honest effort. They know I am asking only for something they can deliver consistently, and they respect me for making that fair demand of them. When they deliver, they earn deserved approval and get self-worth in return, regardless whether they win or not.

I have to admit that there is a bit of a selfish motivation in my wanting the teams I coach to do well. I know that the way the team performs reflects on me as a coach, as a woman, and as a little person. Like anyone who takes up coaching—or any other endeavor—I want the respect of my peers. But I also know that I face hurdles that most coaches don't face, the first being that I am a little person who has never played the game, and the second being that I am a woman coaching a boys' team.

I try not to be oversensitive to the ill-informed first impressions people have or to the fact that they often underestimate me. I understand that their conceptions come from a lack of information and from the stereotypes people have been fed throughout their lives.

I have to say that there is nothing more gratifying to me when I see up close and personal the evidence that I have earned people's respect in the coaching arena. For example, after one game, an opposing coach came up to me in the parking lot and struck up a conversation. "You know," he said, "I have some questions for you." He then went on to tell me that he was having a hard time getting certain members of his team to understand defensive strategies. Then he asked me for some advice on how to get the kids to understand their roles on the team when it came to playing defense.

Wow! I thought. *He's asking* me! I don't know if he saw in me someone who knew a lot about soccer—and honestly, I'm no expert—but I do know that he saw how I talked to my team and how they played and behaved on the field. He saw those things, and he figured he could learn something about coaching soccer from me. Perhaps that something was the coordinated teamwork, defensive or offensive, that comes when players and coaches treat one another with mutual respect.

That showed me something about earning the respect of others, namely that if you do a good job at something, no matter what it might be, people will recognize it and respect you—no matter what your stature, your physical appearance, your gender, or any other factor people tend to focus on.

That is a lesson I try to pass along to all four of my children, and it is my hope that they know that it's not people's shallow first impressions of them that count but what they are capable of doing. On a team, that means working together to reach the goal (literally), but you do that by showing mutual respect for everyone's abilities, be they large or small, and fitting every player's strengths into a winning strategy.

Amy says:

People will come to conclusions about what you are capable of based on your height, your gender, and other factors. Oftentimes, a big part of earning people's respect is showing them that those things don't matter as much as the passion it takes to learn what you are doing and to become good at it. Others will recognize your effort and reward you with respect, but be sure you recognize their efforts and reward them with your respect. Then everybody wins.

FIGHTING ASSUMPTIONS AND EXCEEDING EXPECTATIONS

Matt

It was a long time ago in my life that I had gotten used to that look people give me the first time they see me—see that I am not only little but that I have a difficult time just getting around because of the condition of my joints and limbs. I understand why folks give the look, even though I don't need and don't want what that look is saying.

It's a look of pity. It's a look that says, in so many words, that they feel sorry for me because of my condition, that they can't believe someone who looks like me and who struggles with so many day-to-day tasks that most people take for granted could actually be a happy, well-balanced, productive human being.

I saw the look recently at a sales engagement I was invited to take part in, one that included Fortune 500 companies. I was there not just because I sell computer software but because I'm a very good software salesman. In other words, I was there because I get the job done!

This particular company had spent a fair amount of money to fly their people in from all over the world to take a look at what we and other companies had to offer them.

I am part of a sales team that includes salesmen who mostly have the classic salesman look—tall, dark, and handsome. And then there's me—obviously not tall, clearly not dark, and not the kind of guy who even slightly leans toward handsome.

First, I felt the looks of pity because of my physical condition and appearance. But that was followed by something I hadn't felt thrown my way in a long time. It was a look that said, "The only reason the little guy is here is that they are trying to fill a quota or to have some kind of diversity on the sales team."

After I'd spent more than twenty years in the industry!

I knew I had to be careful as I began taking part in this sales meeting. If there's one thing any physically challenged person—or any person who is "different" in any way—knows, it's that you can't jump in and come on too strong because you want to overcome what others are thinking about you. You have to pick and choose your times carefully and wait until the opportunity to prove yourself presents itself. In sports parlance, you have to let the game come to you.

That's exactly what I did.

Little by little, I did what I do well at this meeting, and in a short time I was able to contribute in a way so meaningful that during lunch break one of the chief executives of the company we were doing our presentation for pulled me aside, shook his head in disbelief, and very sincerely complimented my contribution and indicated I had added significant value to the presentation.

I don't know if I performed any better—or any worse—

than the others on my sales team that day, and I don't really care about that. I know that I did the job the best I could that day, and because of that I made an impression on someone who obviously hadn't known quite what to expect from me.

You can't control much about the first impression you make as a little person, but you can choose how you react. You can control the quality of work you do and the way you carry yourself in every situation.

That's a lesson I've applied to my life, and it's one I want my children to understand.

> *Matt says:*
> *Gaining respect often means fighting the assumptions of others based on your appearance simply by doing what you are hired to do, doing it well, and allowing the results to speak for themselves.*
>
>

RESPECT FOR
MY BROTHER

Jeremy

My parents are big on respect. When they see us slip up with them, other adults, our friends, strangers, or one another, we're sure to hear about it. It's the reap-what-you-sow story. If you don't show respect, how can you expect to get it? One of the things I respect about my parents is that they give me the room to make my own decisions, even when I might make the wrong one.

For the most part, I think we do a good job of showing our parents respect. We appreciate the things they do for us, and we do what they tell us to do (most of the time), even when it doesn't make sense to us. And, of course, we admire and respect the things they have done to get where they are today.

Because your brothers or sister make you mad doesn't mean you don't respect them. Sure, we argue sometimes, and we may even say ugly things to one another now and again. I know I have, and I always feel bad about it. And just because I look down on them, being the oldest and tallest, doesn't mean I don't look up to them too. Just ask me if I'd trade them for any of their friends.

I have particular respect for my twin brother, Zachary,

because he does things above and beyond what people think he can do. In most ways, I don't see Zachary as being any different from anyone else. He's just my brother. But I have to say that when I see him drive the tractor, tough it out after an operation, or go one-on-one with someone twice his size on the soccer field I have a whole new level of respect for him. He's one of the toughest people I know—in mind and body—and he gets the most out of what God has given him. He never backs down from anyone or anything, either on the soccer field or in life.

I do get angry at Zachary sometimes, just like brothers do with one another. But I always feel respect for him. It's not just that he is my brother and a human being. I also respect him because he's a good guy who does things a lot of little people wouldn't even try. I don't see him as small or as anything but my twin brother, my friend, and my teammate.

Having a little person as a brother taught me something else about respect: Treat everyone as they deserve to be treated. Just about every year I get to go to the annual Little People of America National Convention, an event I always look forward to.

There are all kinds of fun activities at the LPA convention—parties, dances, athletic events, and all kinds of music and other entertainment. I always have fun watching Zachary playing basketball and soccer at the Dwarf Athletic Association of America Games, held at the same time.

As a tall person, I have a little bit of an advantage at the convention because everyone there knows me. That's part of why I am so comfortable talking to the people there and why it's OK for me to spend a lot of my time there either hunched down or on my knees so that I can see eye to eye with the little people there and more easily talk to them and hear them talking to me.

I've been asked several times if I'm ever worried that someone might take it wrong, that they might think I was being disrespectful. But most of the people there know me (it helps that Dad was once the LPA president) and they know that I'd never do anything to be insulting or to be a wise guy. In fact, they know that if I don't kneel down—or at least crouch down—I'd be the odd man out in all the social events because I might not be able to hear what people were saying, and if anyone understands being the odd man out it's little people.

Having been around little people all my life, I know there are certain things you can and can't do and say when you first meet someone. I know that if I was going to my first LPA convention and didn't know anyone, there's no way I would kneel down like that. But because so many of the people there know me and know I'm a respectful person, I don't have to worry about offending anyone. All I have to do is be myself.

Jeremy says:
Respect for your family often means
showing enthusiasm for their interests and
also respect for those they respect.

Roloff Family Value #5
Family Pride

Amy

IF YOU'RE GOING TO have a strong family unit, you need a lot of things, including those twin values of love and commitment we've already discussed. But there is another Roloff family value that underlies both love and commitment, and it's that sense of family pride.

In the family context, *pride* means that each of us—

Matt and I, as well as our children—puts the other five members of the family in a place of esteem high enough that we will be willing to stand up for each other above anyone else.

One thing family pride is not, at least in the Roloff family, is an attitude of arrogance or an air that we are better than anyone else—as a family or as individuals. We try to instill in each of our kids—and ourselves—a sense of humility, which I would define as not thinking more highly of yourself than you should and not thinking you are better than anyone.

Before you start thinking that we're some abnormally closed family unit that has no life outside the home, let me clarify. Each of us has good and important friends outside the family, friends we love and cherish. But none of us would ever think of putting any of our friends, no matter how dear they are, before the members of our family.

Matt and I both know how easy it could be for our kids, especially as they get older, to be ashamed of or embarrassed by our family—or at least to worry about what their friends will think when they first see that Mom and Dad are both little people. And believe us, we are well aware that seeing us for the first time will turn a kid's head!

First of all, nearly all teenagers—even those with averaged-sized, good-looking parents—go through that stage where they'd just as soon avoid having their friends meet their parents. But in our home, we have never felt like our children were in any way embarrassed or concerned about what people thought about their having two little people for parents. In fact, they are genuinely proud to have us as their mom and dad.

This family pride is reflected in the fact that all of our children are very comfortable in inviting their friends to our home, where they are welcome to spend time, have fun, and relax. (OK, maybe Matt likes to pick on them a little bit, but most of them are comfortable enough in our home to know how to take it.) For those kids who are having a tough time at home or at school, our home is a sanctuary where they can regroup, think, and feel encouraged.

I think I more or less inherited this sense of pride from my own family, because that's where I felt such love and loyalty as I was growing up. I loved my family—my parents, my siblings, my grandparents—and was proud to be a part of their family. As I got older, I began hoping that someday I'd have a family of my own. Now I think that there is an element of family pride in being able to have children, and I feel both proud and blessed to have four wonderful children. The time when I feel the strongest sense of pride is when I hear them talk and interact with other kids and adults alike.

If you want to nurture an atmosphere of family pride in your home, give your kids a reason to feel it. And there is nothing that will do that more than giving them a sense of security in knowing Mom and Dad love each other and their children deeply and unconditionally. Matt and I have had the typical marital ups and downs, but we have been able to hold our family together and to give our kids a sense of belonging.

Matt and I love the fact that our kids are so deeply

devoted to and proud of one another and of us as parents. While we love having them all come home to us every day, we still look forward to a time when they will look back on their years growing up with pride in the fact that they lived in a home where they were loved deeply, accepted unconditionally, and made to feel valued and important.

LEARNING FAMILY PRIDE
FROM THE BEST

Matt

One of the things I learned as a boy was the importance of having your parents let you know that they were proud of you. It's something that was instilled in me and something I try to practice with my kids to this day.

My father was an athletic, tough-guy ex-Marine who no doubt went into his marriage with Mom believing that he would be the father of boys who were just like him. And while he believed his boys would be strong and healthy, he ended up being the father of one healthy daughter and three sons who were severely physically limited in what they could do.

My sister, Ruthi, was the first of Dad and Mom's four children, and she was tall and very athletic. But for my parents, that was the end of producing healthy children. After Ruth, I came along, and it was obvious from the day I was born that I was going to require some extra attention. Two years after me came Joshua, and again, Dad and Mom faced more childbirth trauma, because Josh was born with a severe heart and lung defect, which would ultimately take his life. After Joshua came Sam, who had the same genetic condition with slightly different complications. He had all the same basic characteristics I had: short limbs and deformed joints.

That was the beginning of more than a quarter century of difficulties and trials for my parents. It wasn't easy on them, and, as Dad once said, "I didn't sign up for this!" when he decided to marry and have children.

But while Dad didn't sign up for what fatherhood had brought him, he took to it as well as anyone could have. Dad not only smothered us with genuine fatherly love and affection, he also gave us the strong sense that he was proud of us and proud of everything we did.

I remember as a child wondering how this big, strong, athletic guy could be proud of three sons who could barely get around on our own. *Does he really mean it?* I wondered. But he really did. Every chance he had, Dad would tell us how proud of us he was.

That made a big difference in my life and, I believe, in the lives of my brothers. It was because of Dad's words of acceptance and encouragement that I was able to learn a sense of self-worth and dignity—even pride in myself and in my family.

No, Dad didn't sign up for having kids of such limited physical abilities, but he rose to the occasion in every way and took on the job every day with vigor and enthusiasm. It seemed as if raising three boys like us—and doing it so well—was a badge of honor he was proud to wear.

I try to be the source of encouragement to my kids that my father was to me, though I know I'm nowhere near as good about that as he was. But my father instilled in me the importance of letting your kids know that you're proud of them, and it's something I try to do every chance I get.

Matt says:
A big part of building family pride is making sure that you let those who are close to you know that you are proud of who they are and what they do.

FEELING MY SON'S PRIDE
THAT I'M "MOM"

Amy

I don't think there is any better feeling for a mother than to know that your son not only loves you but is also proud to call you "Mom" in front of his friends. That, more than anything, is how I want my children to see me and respond to me when their friends are around.

For the most part, that is the kind of acceptance, love, and family pride I feel coming from my kids. Sure, there are times when they want to have some time with their buddies away from the prying eyes and ears of Mom and Dad. But there are also plenty of times when they tell and show their friends that I'm their mom, that they love me, and that they're proud to be a part of the Roloff family.

I remember well an example of that. Zachary was in the living room with his friends, just talking the way teenagers talk. These were boys he had known—and so had I—since kindergarten. Having never been a sixteen-year-old boy myself, I was curious what they were talking about. It wasn't like I was eavesdropping or "butting in" (although I have been known to do that from time to time); I openly walked in the room and sat down and listened in.

Zachary knew that I was listening—after all, he could see that I was there—but he didn't respond like so many teenagers do. He didn't try to brush me off or tell me to leave him and his friends alone so they could engage in teenager talk. Instead, he allowed me to listen in and even included me in the conversation.

I enjoyed listening and even offering my two cents to Zachary's friends . . . when the timing seemed right. After all, as his mom I'm always concerned about what kind of friends he has, and luckily, they are good kids, just like my son. But what I enjoyed more was what Zachary said to me later on: "Mom, you did great!"

I didn't quite know what to make of that. All I did was sit and listen to some teenaged boys talking, and that didn't seem like anything so great to me. I wanted to know what he meant, so I asked him.

Zachary smiled at me and said, "You came in and didn't start asking questions or saying a lot too soon. You just hung out like you were one of our friends."

There was something very gratifying to me about having my son tell me, in so many words, that he was proud of me. I know that I've always made it a point to tell the kids that I'm proud of them when they do or say good things or when they demonstrate a good attitude about something.

I want that to be a two-way street, though. And to have my son tell me he was proud of me told me that we are well on our way to being the kind of family who not only lives together, plays together, prays together, and gets through every day together, but also one who happily says the good things each of us needs to hear now and again.

> *Amy says:*
> Family pride means being proud to be
> seen with one another, proud to claim one
> another, and proud to tell one another how
> you feel. Parents and kids alike should take
> the time to say, "I'm proud of you!"
>
>

PRIDE IN A LITTLE MOM

Amy

One time I took my kids to the local shopping mall, and one little girl saw me with my children and cried out to her mother, "Mom, she's a little mom!" That was followed by the horrified and red-faced mother's correction of "Don't say things like that! Let's go!" as she hurried the child away from the scene of the crime.

I have learned not to be offended when things like that happen. In fact, it's almost gotten to the point where I don't notice it most of the time. I know and understand that little people are just something folks don't see every day, and it's bound to get their attention—I'm sure most people would also look twice if they saw someone who was seven foot six walking in the mall. Besides, I can't really be offended because I *am* a "little mom"!

While Matt and I don't pay a lot of attention to that kind of thing, our children—especially our only daughter, Molly—have often taken note of the looks and the things people have done and said when they see us. It's hard for her to understand because we are her mom and dad and this is what we look like. Sometimes she'll even say things to those who stare or ask questions. Molly once answered an inquisitive little girl's question about what was "wrong" with me by snapping at her, "Are you crazy? She's a little mom! Can't you see that?"

It all seemed so simple to our Molly.

Molly

Sometimes it just surprises me that some people don't understand that there are little people in the world and that there are three of them in my family. I get really tired of some of the dumb questions people ask me. Sometimes I just want to say, "Yeah, my mom and dad are short. So what? Now ask me something else!"

They want to know what it's like having two little people as parents. As if I would know of anything else! I have wondered sometimes what it's like to have average-height people for a mom and dad, but I'd never want to change. I love Mom and Dad the way they are, and I'm happy and proud of the kind of parents they've been to me.

I remember one time how a girl in my school came up to me and told me that she was afraid of my mother the first time she saw her. I guess that's because she had never seen a little person before. That's hard for me to understand because I've not only grown up in a home with three little people, but I've also spent so much time around other little people—like my uncle Sam and all the others I've met when we go to the Little People of America conventions and other meetings where there are lots of little people.

Amy

One of the things I tell Molly and the other kids is that they have to understand that we are probably not only the only little people their friends know but maybe even the only ones they've ever seen. That's why they are curious, and that's why they look at us all the time, and that's why they ask what seem to Molly like really dumb questions, because she loves her family and is proud of each and every one of us, short or tall.

> *Molly and Amy say:*
> *Family pride means that the members of*
> *your family are who they are—physical*
> *attributes and all—and you accept them*
> *and love them just because they are your*
> *parents, children, or siblings.*
>
>

TAKING PRIDE IN BEING "DIFFERENT"

Jeremy

For the most part, all of my friends at school and my other friends know about my family. They know that Mom and Dad and my twin brother, Zachary, are little people—sometimes they say the word *midgets*, but I always correct that—and that my younger brother, Jacob, and my sister, Molly, are both average-sized like me.

Not long ago, Dad looked up at me and asked me if any of my friends or other people I know have ever given me a hard time about my family. I just looked at him and said, "Are you kidding me? They wouldn't dare! I'm Jeremy Roloff!"

I know Dad and Mom like it that I'm proud of our family. I'm proud of the kind of parents they are and the things they've overcome to accomplish what they have. But when I look at my family and how different it looks from almost any other family, I can't help but feel some pride in the fact that we *are* so different.

I just think it's cool being apart from the norm. Being a half-small, half-tall family makes life here on the farm more fun and exciting. I love the way my family is, and I wouldn't have it any other way.

I have had people ask me if I've ever wondered what it would be like to have a family in which everyone is average-sized. Of course, I do wonder about that—you always wonder what it would be like if things in your life were different than they are—but I still wouldn't trade what I have in this family for anything.

I'm proud of Dad because he has had to overcome so much to be successful at the things he's done. He's not just a little person but a little person with a lot of physical problems, yet he hasn't let that stop him from doing the things he wants to do in life.

I'm proud of Mom because she is a great mother who loves her children and would do anything for us. She's not only our mom but she's also a soccer coach and a preschool teacher, and those are both things to be proud of.

I'm proud of my twin brother, Zachary, because he works so hard at being a good soccer player, even though as a little person he can't run up and down the field as fast as some people. But he won't quit, and so he does good things on the field.

And I'm proud of Molly and Jacob, because they, like me, are proud to be part of a family that is so different!

> *Jeremy says:*
> *Part of family pride is enjoying the
> differences between your family and other
> people's families. Every family has its own
> unique qualities, and those are the things
> that make your family your family.*

THE PRIDE AND LOYALTY
OF A BROTHER

Zachary

When you live with a family like mine—three little people and three average-sized people—there can be some pretty fun and funny moments when we're out doing the things we do every day.

My brother Jeremy has always been great about letting people know that I'm his brother and about letting them know that he's not going to put up with people making fun of me or teasing me because I'm a little person. If that were to happen, he'd certainly say something about it. He'd do that for any member of our family. We hang out together at school with the same group of friends, and he always includes me in whatever he and the rest of our friends are doing.

Jeremy and I are both proud of each other and of our family. We're proud of what our mother and father have done here and how they've made a thirty-four-acre farm the cool place to be for all our friends.

People at school look up to Jeremy because he's a great soccer player, and he uses that to his advantage when it comes to sticking up for me. I play on the same high school team as Jeremy. I'm not the best player on the team—that would be Jeremy—but I'm also not the worst.

I know it can be kind of shocking to see a little person playing high school soccer with a bunch of average-sized guys, and sometimes I feel the looks or hear the little comments. Some of the kids we play against can't believe I'm out there, and they say so.

Jeremy sticks up for me on the soccer field by making smart-aleck comments to the players he knows are being disrespectful toward me, and he usually does it out loud so everyone knows who said it. He also calls me "Bro" on the field, so that everyone knows that I'm not just his friend or teammate but also his brother.

In one game, we were getting beat pretty bad, and the guys on the team that was beating us were doing a lot of talking. But I had a chance to make a steal and make a great pass against a player who had been mouthing off. It was a pretty sweet move. Jeremy just couldn't leave it alone. "What's this?" he yelled out. "You guys are getting schooled by a dwarf?" I couldn't stop laughing, but I also appreciated Jeremy's sticking up for me and letting people know he was proud of the play I'd made.

> *Zachary says:*
> You can show pride in and loyalty to your family in all kinds of settings and in all kinds of ways. And doing so can also bring you closer.
>
>

BALANCING PRIDE
WITH HUMILITY

Peggy

One of the hardest balances to strike when you're raising children, especially those with severe physical limitations, is the one between a healthy sense of pride and self-respect and a self-absorbed, arrogant egomania.

If you were to ask Matt, he'd tell you that his father was the one who was charged with the responsibility of building up his self-esteem and self-respect, and I was the one who was in charge of keeping him humble. In other words, Ron would set Matt up, and I'd knock him down a few pegs.

In truth, I was always concerned that Matt and his brothers maintain a good self-image and that they approach life and people alike with a sense of confidence in themselves, that sense that told them they were as good as other people—even though their bodies weren't as healthy.

At the same time, though, I knew how important it would be for Matt to somehow remain humble. I tried my best to temper the positive self-image we instilled in him with a real spirit of humility.

In our home, the Bible was a big part of the teachings

and encouragements we'd give our boys. And I would often read to our sons what the Good Book had to say about pride. "Pride comes before a fall," the Bible tells us in Proverbs 16:18. And in the New Testament, we read, "God gives grace to the humble" (James 4:6). That list could go on and on, but the point would remain the same: if we want God to do good things for us and in us, we need to remain humble.

There is a good pride, a good kind of self-respect, and it is the kind we tried to instill in Matt and the kind he tries to instill in his own children. It's a pride that says that you have value despite the fact that you have a physical limitation, despite the fact that you walk on crutches, despite the fact that in a lot of ways it doesn't seem like life has been fair to you.

On the other hand, there is the kind of pride and self-image we tried to discourage in Matt and in his brothers, and that's the arrogant kind of pride, the kind where they saw themselves as being more than they really were. Sometimes, we would point out people who were arrogant or overly proud or boastful, and we'd tell the boys, "You don't want to be like that. Nobody likes someone who brags on himself all the time." And I'd often tell Matt, "You'd better be careful, or you won't be able to get your head through the door."

Sometimes it seemed as though that message was falling on deaf ears. Matt had quite the ego; there were times when he seemed like a peacock or a little banty rooster strutting around the barnyard looking for trouble. He has mellowed with age—though he still believes that I'm in his life to keep him humble—and has become a more humble person.

I believe that Matt and Amy do a wonderful job of

balancing their kids' need for positive self-esteem with their need for true humility.

I know that they also discourage the children from bragging. When one of the kids wants to talk about something good he or she has done, Matt tells them to keep that "bragging" in the home and not take it to their friends. As parents they understand the pitfalls that the kids risk through becoming boastful or proud—namely that nobody will want to be around them.

It's never easy to instill in a child a sense of self-worth and self-respect while at the same time teaching him or her to be humble. But that is exactly what Matt and Amy are doing with their four children now.

Peggy says:

It's always important for parents to instill in their children a healthy sense of self-respect and self-confidence, but it's just as important that they teach their children to be humble. Their children will demonstrate respect for themselves and for others.

Roloff Family Value #6
The Importance of Parenting

Matt

I HAVE HAD A great life in just about every way. I have incredible parents who made what would otherwise have been unbearable, bearable. I enjoy a great career where I've been successful and able to support myself and my family. And I enjoy being married to a wonderful, beautiful woman who I call the tail to my kite and the rudder to my ship.

One of the best things about being married to Amy—and there are many—is that we've had the wonderful privilege and the solemn responsibility of becoming Mom and Dad to Jeremy, Zachary, Jacob, and Molly.

I never cease to be amazed at the depth of love I have for these kids. I love them more than I can adequately put into words, and there is nothing I wouldn't do to make sure that they are cared for, protected, and comfortable.

As far as we know, we are the only little people parents who have had four kids naturally, and we're one of a very few who have had twins. But that isn't what strikes us most about being the parents of four children. What delights us is watching each of our children grow—physically, emotionally, socially, and spiritually.

Our children are growing up to be unique individuals. Each of them has the same two parents, and yet their personalities are all very different. Yes, there are some similarities, but there are far more differences. They aren't perfect children—none are—but they are all great kids who have their own talents, gifts, and personality traits, all of which combine to make them the individuals they are.

But none of these things has happened by accident. They are partly the result of our constant effort to be the best parents possible. Amy and I have enjoyed watching our children grow. And as we continue allowing them to grow in their thinking and in their talents and skills, we look forward to seeing even more growth as the result of this active parenting as they become young adults, and especially when they become parents themselves. We hope our kids will have seen the value of our efforts with them and someday do the same with their own children.

GIVING MY CHILDREN
WHAT I NEVER HAD

Matt

I won't deny that in many ways I felt a little gypped as a child because I missed out on so many things that typical kids get to enjoy. I can remember many summers being laid up in body casts and braces hearing and watching the neighborhood kids outside running, playing, and chasing one another around, just like kids do.

There were the times when I did some of those things myself, but they were few and far between. That is part of why I became determined from a very young age to give my children the things I couldn't have. When Amy first got pregnant with Jeremy and Zach, I was determined to give them not just what I didn't have as a kid, but what I would call the ultimate childhood.

When we found out that Amy was pregnant, we were living in San Jose, California, in the heart of Silicon Valley, where I was working hard to make a future for us. We lived in a nice home but one with a very small backyard—hardly big enough for our boys to have the kinds of childhood adventures I wanted them to have. One of the things that motivated Amy and me to move to Oregon was that I felt that we needed a much bigger canvas, in terms of real estate, to paint that childhood for my kids.

The ultimate childhood I envisioned wasn't one made of plastic or one you can plug into a wall socket. It wasn't one of video games and iPods and computers. Those things have their places in our kids' lives, but I had a much different vision—a *bigger* vision—one where the kids could enjoy the same adventures as Tom Sawyer and the Hardy Boys and others I had read about as I lay in hospital beds or in my own bedroom watching and hearing kids do the things I longed to be doing myself.

This was a vision of a king-sized playground filled with the kinds of adventures even the healthiest kids I knew when I was a child could only dream of. It was a place where there were tracks for them to ride their tricycles and bicycles on, where they could run and play and never feel crowded, where there were more trees than they could climb or build houses in. I wanted them to have the opportunity to build, to create, and to enjoy the very best that being a kid has to offer.

I built my ultimate backyard playground for the kids and had a blast doing it—kind of a second childhood for me but playing with real backhoes and tractors this time. When the kids go flying along the zip line or splash from the pirate ship into the pond, it makes all the work pay off. I'm not even sure I should call it work. Just making it was my splash in the pond.

I thank God every day for the opportunity and

privilege of being a dad, and I make sure the kids know it. And while I'm not a perfect father and never claimed to be, I am a father who wants his kids to enjoy all the good things childhood brings with it.

> *Matt says:*
> *Being a parent means giving our children the things we may have missed out on as kids. In doing that, we get to enjoy through them what we couldn't enjoy for ourselves.*
>
>

TELLING THE TRUTH IN LOVE—
EVEN WHEN IT'S TOUGH

Amy

I think it's natural for a mom to want to protect her children from any kind of hurt—either physical or emotional. I know that Peggy, Matt's mother, has said many times that she would never change how Matt and our family have turned out but that she would have wanted to spare him the pain he went through because of all the surgeries and recoveries he had to endure.

Sometimes, though, the motherly instincts and affection I have for my children when it comes to keeping them from getting hurt run headlong into the need for them to know the truth, even when it hurts. I don't want my children to get hurt, but I also don't want to keep the truth from them, because to do that is not only dishonest but also unloving.

I became concerned about a situation several years back in which one of the girls Zach and Jeremy go to school with began calling Zach on the phone. They were in fourth or fifth grade at the time.

I sensed that while the girl wasn't trying to "use" Zach (she was just a kid and didn't think in those terms anyway), she wasn't as interested in him as she was in his brother.

That's not to say that Zach isn't a likable kid or that there aren't girls who like him—there certainly are! But I think more than anything this girl viewed Zach as a friend and believed that it was OK to talk to him to find out more about Jeremy. In truth, I knew she would have been more interested in Jeremy simply because she was an average-sized person, and most of the time average-sized people are attracted to others who are close to their own height.

At that point, I was faced with a dilemma. I wanted to be honest with Zach because I knew that my not being honest could increase the chances of his being hurt. On the other hand, I didn't want to hurt his feelings and make him feel like he was being used. I believed that the girl liked him, but as a friend.

Finally, I came to the conclusion that Zach was far better off hearing the truth from me than he was believing this girl had an interest in him she didn't have only to find out it was Jeremy she wanted to get to know better. I didn't want him to feel shocked and hurt or to think she was being mean to him.

I sat Zach down and talked to him about the girl and her phone calls. I was as gentle but as direct and honest as I could be when I told him, "You know, Zach, she does like you and likes talking to you. But don't be surprised if her real purpose in calling you is to talk to Jeremy."

I wasn't sure if Zach fully understood what I was trying to tell him that day, but just a few days later the same girl called again. She made some small talk with him for a while, then I saw the look on his face. His eyes got big as he seemed to realize that what I had told him was true.

The girl had finally disclosed her motives. He later told me that she had asked him, "Can I talk to Jeremy?"

Zachary was OK with her wanting to talk to his brother, and I think it was because I had prepared him for what was coming that he wasn't badly hurt.

Amy says:
Sometimes, being a parent means telling your child the truth as you see it, even if it might not be comfortable to hear.

THE KIND OF PARENT
I WANT TO BE

Jeremy

One of the funnest memories I have of Dad and living on the farm is going on what we call "mule trips." That's when we'd get in the ATV, a Kawasaki "mule" to get around the farm because he can't get that far on his crutches, and we'd just drive around the farm during the summer—through the fields and the trees. Dad loved being out there with us, and I think he had almost as much fun as we did.

That's part of what makes Dad so special. While a lot of fathers love their kids and would do anything for them (and my dad is like that), he also likes to do adventures with us.

Someday, I want to get married and be a dad myself, and I'm not talking about just one child, either. I'd like to have three or four and buy them a farm like the one I've lived on all my life. I also know that there are a lot of things about my mother and father that I'd like to copy when I have children.

People ask if I worry about having children who are little people. I think about that sometimes, and I know that it's possible. I mean, my grandparents on both sides had kids who are dwarfs (Dad's parents had two!), and, of course, my parents had a child who is a dwarf. I know that their condition is genetic and that I have it in my own genes.

But honestly, I'm not worried about that. If I get married someday and have three tall kids, that's great! But if it ends up that one, two, three, or all—however many that may be—of my kids are little people, that's great too, because I've seen in my dad and mom—as well as my uncle Sam, my brother Zachary, and the other little people I've known since I was a kid—that little people can have great lives, even if they do have to overcome some things I haven't had to.

And even though it's not easy being the parent of a little person, I've seen a lot of proof you can do it. The parents just have to love each other and love their kids.

One of the great things about Mom and Dad is that they balance one another out because their personalities are so different. For example, where Dad might be a little more of a dreamer and adventurer, Mom is more practical and tries to keep our heads from getting too far in the clouds. Where Mom might be the one who does the discipline, Dad is the one who encourages us to think and grow and plan for ourselves. It actually makes for a great combination.

From what I've learned from my parents, being a good parent means making sacrifices for your children. I know that both Dad and Mom have made big sacrifices for me and my brothers and sister. And that is one of the reasons I know that they love me. You don't give up everything for someone unless you really love them, and that's what Mom and Dad have done for me in more ways than I can count, starting with building the farm for us.

Mom and Dad don't claim to be perfect parents. Sometimes when they punish me or discipline me, I know I have it coming. But sometimes they do or say things or make me do things I don't think are fair or right, and that makes me mad. But they are my parents and I love them, and I know that the things they do and make me do—even when I think they are wrong—are for my benefit because they want what is best for me in every area of life. I know that's what they're doing even when we disagree on what's right.

I hope someday when I have kids that they can look at the kind of dad I am and honestly say the same things about me.

Jeremy says:
Being a good mom and dad means enjoying being with your kids and making sacrifices for them. It also means disciplining them, even when they don't think the way you do it is right or fair.

Roloff Family Value #7
An Attitude of Optimism

Matt

I DON'T KNOW WHO said it or under what circumstances, but there is a saying I think demonstrates one of the most important values we hold dearly in the Roloff home: "Those who say they can and those who say they can't have one thing in common: they're both right."

Optimism to me means having a positive attitude

that says no matter how difficult things get, I can and will bounce back and make good things happen for myself and for my family.

This is one area where Amy and I are very different in our approach to life. While Amy certainly believes in having a positive attitude, she is also one whose optimism is almost always tempered by the realism of our situation. While I may look at a pile of bills and a bank account statement that reads "empty" and say that things are about to get better, Amy will look at that same situation, acknowledge that we could be in trouble, and ask, "What are we doing about this?"

To put it another way, we're both glass-half-full people, but while I tend to focus on what I believe is the fact that the glass will be filled to the brim, Amy tends to look at *how* the glass will be filled or what we are doing to make sure that happens.

To Amy, optimism means having the ability not to wallow in or focus on what is wrong but instead having the mental toughness to think through your situation and either get yourself out of it or make it better. When you lose that sense of optimism, then you lose some of your ability to figure out how to fix things. When that happens, you get yourself in a slump you can't pull yourself out of.

This doesn't mean that you don't recognize that you are in a bad situation. It just means that you acknowledge that you are in that situation and that you don't like being in it, but you still have the ability to remain positive and know that something better is going to come along.

Like so many of the values in this book, I learned

optimism early in life. For me, it was a matter of survival. I can't tell you that I spent all that time recovering from surgeries as a child with a smile on my face, feeling optimistic. I shed a lot of tears and endured a lot of pain back then, and I even had some times when I thought it wasn't fair that I should be lying in bed while other kids were out playing and exploring and just being kids.

What got me through all that was a pair of extraordinarily optimistic parents who, although they went through their share of anguish over our situation, supported me, smiled at me, and let me know that no matter how rough things got, it would get better. It worked, too. I can remember thinking after my parents had finished encouraging me, *Hey, one day I will get out of here and do things. It's not going to be like this forever.*

It would have been easy for me to give in to negativity back then, but because I didn't, and because Mom and Dad wouldn't allow me to wallow in self-pity and negativity, I have become the kind of person who now finds it easy to have an attitude of optimism in even the direst of situations and circumstances.

To me, that is an example of something I've come to believe about attitude: positive or negative, attitude is something you learn. Yes, some people are more predisposed or wired because of their basic personalities to respond in certain ways to certain situations, but I still believe that just about anyone can learn to respond to even the worst of situations optimistically.

One thing I've learned about optimism is that it is like a magnet. By that I mean it tends to attract other good things as well as other people. When you have a positive, upbeat attitude, it will rub off on other people and good things will happen between you and them. People naturally want to be a part of what someone who is optimistic is doing, sometimes because it's pleasant to be around a positive person and sometimes because they draw encouragement from it that can be applied to their own life situations.

On the other hand, if you have a negative attitude, an attitude of "poor me," then people will pick up on that and begin feeling the same way, and sometimes they will just not want to be around you. Nothing good comes of that!

Both Amy and I have done everything we can to instill in our children an attitude of optimism, an attitude that they can do anything they set their minds to if they apply themselves. And while some of the Roloff family values we have included in this book might not work for everyone— at least the way they do for us—we are confident that this one will.

We've never tried to teach our kids that life is always easy, because it isn't. We know our children—like their parents have—will face their own trials. But we've taught them that they can be filled with optimism, because no matter what we as a family have to go through, we're going to go through it together.

STAYING POSITIVE WHEN LIFE SAYS "NO!"

Zachary

In my home, Mom and Dad don't allow us kids to become depressed or discouraged because they don't allow us to feel sorry for ourselves when things don't go our way. When I was told that I couldn't play on the high school soccer team, I didn't let it depress me. Instead I just spent time with my family and friends and played soccer as much as I could with them. I looked at the things I did have and felt confident that good things would happen for me.

I know a lot of people when they don't get what they want, or when someone says they can't do something, tend to just give up and become negative. They figure that if they fail at something or are told they can't do it, there is no point in trying again. But that isn't the way things are in my life or in my family. Instead of assuming that things will never get better just because they didn't work out before, I have to stay upbeat, knowing that if I do, I may get a shot. On the other hand, if I just give up, then nothing good will happen for me.

Like my brothers and sister, I've learned to have a positive attitude from my father. While we are both little people, Dad has been through far more than I have physically and has a far more messed-up body than I do. Yet he has always remained positive and has done a lot of great things for himself and for his wife and children. When I see how positive he has remained, it makes it easier for me to adopt the same kind of attitude.

Mom and Dad have always taught me that life isn't perfect and that sometimes you won't get what you want. But they have also taught me that no matter what happens, I have to remember that there is a purpose for me in everything that happens and that I need to remain positive and have an attitude that things will get better.

> *Zachary says:*
> *It's good to remain positive and optimistic,*
> *because if you aren't, you might miss*
> *opportunities right in front of you.*
>
>

LEARNING TO TEMPER
MY OPTIMISM

Matt

When I lost my high-tech job after 9/11 and became president of the LPA I realized that I had allowed my priorities to get out of balance, something I regret to this day. I wasn't spending enough time with Amy and the kids or tending to their needs, and I wasn't tending to our finances as well as I should have. It wasn't long before our resources began to dry up and we were in trouble.

Amy gave me all the rope I needed to hang myself, but I almost ended up hanging myself and my family along with me. I suddenly awoke to find my family in a very difficult financial situation, so difficult that there was a possibility we could lose the farm. Obviously, I needed to reprioritize and make some changes—and in a hurry.

Though I knew I had messed up—and I confessed as much to Amy—I maintained a positive, optimistic attitude. Somehow, I knew that we were going to pull through and that we were going to be in even better financial shape than before. At that point, it didn't matter as much to me how we got where we were, only that I didn't wallow in blame and self-pity. *We are going to dig our way out,* I thought. *I know things are going to be fine—better than fine.*

I realized I had put Amy through things she shouldn't have had to endure, and one of them came because I didn't simply acknowledge the bind we were in. Amy tried to maintain her own sense of optimism in the midst of a bad period for us, but I only went halfway with her—maintaining the optimism but not acknowledging to and with her the seriousness of our situation.

My instinct when things are difficult is to just see it as part of life, and a part that we will just dig our way out of. But I have learned that while that positive attitude is important for me to maintain, Amy needs for me to acknowledge that things are rough, that we are in a place that I need to use all my resourcefulness and experience to get us out of.

I'm happy to report that once I got my priorities straightened out and started being proactive about our situation, we bounced back with a vengeance. After we "stopped the bleeding" with our finances, we began rebuilding ourselves through faith, hard work, determination, commitment, and, above all, optimism. I went back to work full-time and started my own company, and Amy began working as a preschool teacher in our children's private Christian school.

It was the end of a rough period for Amy and me and the kids, and I am still thankful that we hung together as a family through it all. And I am also thankful that although I made mistakes, our recovery reaffirmed for us the value of optimism even during difficult times.

Matt says:

Optimism—a positive attitude in all things—doesn't mean that you don't acknowledge that things are rough, that you're uncomfortable, or even that you're a little worried about your situation. It simply means that you know that things will get better—as long as you don't give in to self-pity or negativity.

OPTIMISM DURING
A TOUGH TIME

Jeremy

It seems like one of the most important things Dad has taught us Roloff kids is the importance of having a positive attitude. When you think good, positive thoughts, it's more likely that good, positive things will happen in your life. I think that's true in school, with your friends, with activities, and with life in general.

Ever since I can remember, my friends have always told me that I am a positive, optimistic person and that they like being around someone like that. I think that is something I inherited from my dad. He's a very optimistic guy. Even when bad things happen or when someone is sick or in pain, he has a way of looking at the situation in a positive light. I think that either that attitude rubbed off on me from being around him so much or I've inherited it through Dad's genes.

I think one of the reasons Dad is able to be so positive all the time is that, as a little person, he's had to learn to overcome. The only way you can do that without getting discouraged or depressed is to remain positive and not let things get you down. He's almost always positive and optimistic, and that helps everyone around him to be the same way.

That is true of Dad even when bad things happen, like when my twin brother, Zachary, had to have emergency surgery. When Zachary was very young, the doctors had to put what is called a shunt in his head to drain fluid off his brain. It's pretty common for little people to have excess fluid on their brains, and that was the problem with Zachary when he was a little kid. Without a shunt to drain the fluids, this condition could have killed Zachary.

In the past few years, Zach has had to have operations to repair or replace the shunt in his head. Those surgeries were very serious, and without them he could again have died. The amazing thing to a lot of people when Zach was having his operations was how calm and positive everyone in the family was through it all. It would have been easy to feel down when my brother was in the hospital having an operation to save his life, and I wanted to be there for him. But I really wasn't that scared, and that's because Mom and Dad didn't act scared at all. Sure, they were worried and concerned, but it always seemed to us that they were confident that Zachary was going to be fine.

In the same way that we could all have gotten scared and despairing if just one of us was, we all rallied and spurred each other on to stay positive. It's no wonder Zach pulled through and was back to normal within a month.

Jeremy says:
The most important time to have a
positive, optimistic attitude, is often during
life's greatest challenges.

OPTIMISM MEANS SEEING PAST
THE SITUATION

Peggy

One of the qualities we see in our family is optimism in the face of difficulty and suffering. Matt and Amy, who have both endured more than their share of difficulties—in their own lives and in the lives of their children—have done an amazing job of instilling in their kids the idea that no matter how difficult things may get, they can always look forward to better times.

"Zach, hang in there! I know it hurts, but it's going to get better. Believe me, it is going to get better," Amy encouraged Zachary when he had surgery.

Amy understood—and was demonstrating to Zachary—what the Roloff family has learned repeatedly over the years: self-pity just can't cut it in the Roloff family. Yes, you can acknowledge that you are in pain, and you can even cry out over it. But you have to be able to focus on what is ahead, and that there is something better once you have recovered.

Ron and I learned that for ourselves as we raised Sam and Matt. I discovered that you can't just tell a suffering child to "Hang in there" or "Buck up" without giving him something to be hopeful and optimistic about.

Sometimes we're asked if there is anything we would change about our situation if we had the choice. When people ask that, they probably think we're going to smile and say, "We wouldn't change a thing!" But that's just not the way we see our lives. While we wouldn't change the results—a wonderful, loving, healthy family—we might change the way we've arrived here.

No mother or father wants to have their children endure the kind of pain our children and grandchildren have had to go through, and if we could change that, we would. That wasn't an enjoyable experience in any way, and we obviously would rather have avoided the physical pain and emotional suffering the boys had to go through.

But one of the good things to come out of that suffering in the Roloff family is the ability to see past the difficulties in life—past the pain, no matter how terrible it is—and see that it won't always be there, that we will know better times if we can just get through it. And we also see that there is good that can come out of even the worst situations.

When we were in the midst of raising our children, we met people who felt sorry for us and who offered us their sympathy. And while we appreciate where they were coming from, we've realized that although there are things we'd rather have avoided in the past forty years, we couldn't be happier with the results.

When we look at what we've come through as a family, we can feel nothing but gratitude for the results we see before us. We know a lot of people who haven't had to endure a lot of pain, who are financially well off, who have had far easier lives than we have. But the bottom line to us is, we're having the last laugh. We've got ten beautiful grandchildren whom we love more than life itself.

And that is because we as a family have learned what it takes to remain optimistic and to maintain a positive attitude, even during the worst times of suffering.

> *Peggy says:*
> *Having a positive, optimistic attitude*
> *means keeping an eye on that time in the*
> *future when things will be better for you.*
>
>

Roloff Family Value #8
Faith

Matt

AS WE'VE SAID, IN the Roloff home there are some values that are negotiable and some that are more important to Amy than they are to me. But there is one value that we are in 100 percent agreement about, and it's the value called faith.

The word *faith* has come to mean a lot of things to different people. There is faith in others, faith in ourselves, faith in the institutions that are important to us. Those things can be important values to be sure, but the kind of faith Amy and I are talking about here is our deeply held faith in God.

The Bible describes faith this way: "Now faith is being sure of what we hope for and certain of what we do not see" (Hebrews 11:1). I don't think we can describe faith any better than that, but what we can do is tell you that when we talk about faith as a family value, we're talking about the kind of faith whose essence is rooted in three things: believing in a God who keeps his promises, believing in a God who doesn't make mistakes, and believing in a God who is always with us and completely in control of everything—in the very best of times and in the very worst of times.

We talked about the importance of having an optimistic, positive attitude. But ultimately, I don't think it is possible to stay strong and positive without faith, without having that assurance that God is doing something good through everything that happens in your life. Without that kind of faith, tough times are just tough times that don't necessarily make a lot of sense. But I have come to a point where I believe that everything that goes wrong or feels bad or negative has behind it the fact that God is doing something good in my life. *That* is what gives me an attitude of optimism!

Amy and I don't claim to be perfect Christians or perfect in our faith. What we do claim to be are two people who know that without that deep sense of faith in and dependency on God, we wouldn't be able to be the kind of parents we are, have the kind of marriage we have, or enjoy the kind of family life we wake up and thank God for every day.

I personally don't think of myself as the classic "man of God." I often struggle with attitudes and actions I know aren't pleasing to God—attitudes and actions Amy sees up close and personal. But despite my own spiritual and personal struggles, I have never stopped loving God, never stopped believing the things he promises me in the Bible, and never stopped trusting that he will use everything that happens to me—and everything I do—to make me more humble and more dependent on him in every area of my life.

I'm not always faithful to doing and being what God wants, but I know that he is. And I'm absolutely secure in the knowledge that he loves me and is committed to making me more like Christ every day and in every way. I know that God never changes, and he's as dependable now as he ever has been.

Amy and I were both brought up in Christian homes where church was a central part of the family's weekly activities. But more important, both her parents and mine helped us to understand that God had a purpose for our lives, that our being little people was part of that purpose, and that we were made exactly the way we were meant to be.

I guess you could say that faith was a family value instilled in me since I was a baby—maybe even before that. If that sounds strange, bear with me and see if it doesn't make sense.

You see, while I was still in my mother's womb, Mom and Dad had no idea how badly physically challenged I would be, how many surgeries I would have to undergo, how many hours of rehabilitation I would have to endure, or what kinds of hardships they would endure raising me and my brothers and sister.

My parents had no way of knowing any of that before I was born, but what they did know was this: God was and is in control. That faith continued well after I was born. And though they would go through things as parents that most moms and dads can't even begin to understand, they always knew that no matter where parenthood took them, God was going to be there for them every step of the way, giving them the strength, wisdom, and endurance it took to be the kind of parents they were.

Mom and Dad have always instilled that sense of faith in me and my brothers, and that's why, as a small boy and beyond, I knew God was in control. When I was going through the indescribable pain of the surgeries and rehabilitations, God was in control. When I was trying to find my way in school so that I could somehow fit in, God was in control. When I allowed my own youthful stupidity and arrogance to lead me down a path of destructive behavior, God was in control. When I met Amy, married her, and became the father of four beautiful children, God was in control.

God was in control through all of that, and he's still in control now. And though I'm no more certain of what will happen in our lives next than any other husband or father, I know beyond a doubt that God has everything mapped out for me, my wife, and my children. That's why I approach the future with a sense of excitement and not fear, and it's why I am able to keep myself moving toward the ultimate destination God has for me.

That is the sense of faith and trust in God that Amy and I have as parents, the kind we want to instill in our children every day and in every circumstance. We want them to understand that as much as they can count on Mom and Dad to always be there for them, they can depend infinitely more strongly on the love and support of their heavenly Father.

CHALLENGED TO BELIEVE
. . . AND TO ACT

Amy

Sometimes faith looks you right in the eye and asks you whether you are going to follow what you know is right, what you know God wants you to do, even when it means personal hardship and risk you might not otherwise take.

For a little person, getting pregnant and giving birth is always riskier than it is for most average-sized people. That is simply because our bodies are put together differently, making complications more likely than for average-sized women. Most of the time, women who are little have to take extra precautions during pregnancy, and when the day for delivery comes, they have to have cesarean sections in order to help ensure the safety of the baby and the mother.

In my case, my first pregnancy was even riskier than most because I was carrying twins—our sons Jeremy and Zachary. We knew from when we first found out I was pregnant that I would have to have a C-section. We knew of all the risks, but we also knew that God was here for us and that he was going to keep me and our babies safe.

Before I became pregnant, Matt and I had discussed the fact that the odds of our having another little person were probably pretty good. But we both wholeheartedly agreed that if that was what God had in store for us, we were going to be fine with it. After all, we were both little people, and while life as a little person isn't always easy, it has still been good for both of us.

When my doctors discovered that I was pregnant with twins, they talked to us about all the options, all the risks, and the things I would have to do in order to have a healthy, relatively uneventful pregnancy. One of the options they talked about was one I found shocking, and it was to eliminate—to abort—one of the babies before the pregnancy progressed too far.

I didn't blame the doctors for bringing it up; after all, they knew the risks of my carrying twins to term, and they knew that the odds of something happening to me and/or both of the babies were higher than for most women. In my mind, they were doing their jobs, and I appreciated that.

However, for me it was never an option to allow one of my babies to be taken from me that way. Matt and I didn't know whether one or both of them would be little people, and honestly it didn't matter. What we knew was that whatever happened, God was going to be with us, that he was going to bless us and protect us through everything.

The bottom line for us was that we were going to proceed in faith, do what we knew was right, and keep both of our babies to term. If God wanted both of them to be born healthy—and at the time I wholeheartedly believed he did—then he was going to take care of everything for us. In our minds, he had given us this wonderful opportunity, this privilege, to become parents, and we weren't going to do anything short of laying everything about the pregnancy at his feet and allowing him to care for us and our children.

"We are going forward with both of these babies," I remember saying, and I knew I had Matt's full support.

In the end, we were glad we kept our faith, because we were blessed with the arrival of two babies, one of whom was a little person and one of whom was average-sized, both healthy.

Amy says:

Having true faith in God means sticking to your convictions and doing what you believe is right in his eyes, knowing that he is going to take care of you and your family in even the riskiest and most dangerous situations.

WHEN GOD GIVES
A QUALIFIED "YES"

Matt

There has never been a time in my life when I thought of myself as an accident or a fluke or a joke on the part of God. For the most part—and I mean overwhelmingly almost always—I haven't wanted to be anything more or less than God wanted and had made me to be.

I've learned in life that there is great comfort and strength in knowing that you are made for a purpose and that God knows what the purpose is and how to equip you to accomplish it. Not only that, having that sense of purpose has helped me to have an attitude of contentment—even gratitude—over my own physical stature and physical challenges.

I remember, when I was a kid, going to a special church service one evening with my parents in Pengrove, California. It was a fair-sized church, and that night they were holding a healing service. People were walking up to the altar and having the pastor and the elders lay hands on them and pray for physical healing and other needs.

As I sat watching and listening, I wanted more than anything to go down to the altar and get prayed for. I believed with absolute assurance that if I went forward and got someone to pray for me, I would be healed. I wasn't expecting to be able to go to school the next day as tall as everyone else and with my body completely healed. What I did believe is that I would begin the *process* of having my body healed that very night.

"I want to go up there," I told my mother, who was concerned that I might be bitterly disappointed if I were to go up and get prayed for, only to find that my body hadn't changed. But Mom knew better—as do I now—than to stand in the way of a fourth-grade child's demonstration of faith.

Mom still remembers praying for me that night as I got up from my seat, grabbed my crutches, and began walking down the aisle to the altar. She wasn't praying that my body would be healed as much as she was that my heart would be protected against a loss of faith.

As I made my way toward the front of the church, there wasn't a shred of doubt in my mind that a miracle was possible. But not only was a miracle possible, it happened that very night.

But it wasn't the one I thought I was asking for.

The pastor of the church smiled as he put his hands on me and offered up what I knew was a prayer of absolute faith. He asked God to heal me, and I knew at that moment that the prayer had been answered.

If you were to look at me now, you would know that my body wasn't healed that night—or in the years that followed. I'm still short, and my arms, legs, hips, shoulders, and spine are a complete mess and, frankly, getting worse by the year.

But there was something different about me the next day as I got up, had breakfast, and got myself ready for school. No one else could see it—not even Mom—but I knew the pastor's prayers, as well as my own, from the night before had been answered.

I went to school that day still small and walking with the aid of crutches. I had a great day at school, and I couldn't wait to tell Mom about it. "Mom!" I excitedly called out as I walked through the front door of our home. "I think my prayers were answered last night!"

My mother could see that I wasn't any taller and that my body was still deformed. But what she could see as well was that something inside me had changed. God hadn't miraculously healed my body, but he had done something equally amazing. He had given me a sense of acceptance for who I was and how he had made me, and it was a sense I believe the other kids felt too, because for the first time they had invited this disabled, deformed nine-year-old to be a part of their playground games.

Matt says:
It has been said that God answers our prayers in one of three ways: "Yes," "No," and "Not now." But I believe there is a fourth way, and that's to answer us in a way we don't expect and haven't even asked for.

WHEN BAD THINGS HAPPEN
TO GOOD PEOPLE

Peggy

It hasn't been an easy life for my husband and me, and there were times when I didn't know if I could make it. When I was a young mother, I wondered if there was something I had done to deserve what had happened to us. I wondered if giving birth to three boys with severe physical challenges wasn't some kind of punishment from God for some hidden sin.

But as I grew and matured—both as a mother and as a Christian woman—I realized that what had happened wasn't punishment from God at all. I realized he had allowed Ron and me to become parents of these boys so that he could both show his power in very difficult situations and so that he could prepare us to serve him in the ways he had called us to serve him.

Over the years, I've realized that bad things can and do happen to good people and that they happen with the knowledge and permission of a loving God. And I've realized that even when God doesn't answer our prayers to change our situations, he always answers our prayers when we ask him to change us in the middle of those things.

That realization has trickled down to Matt and Amy and to their children. In the Roloff home, there is the underlying understanding that no matter what happens to them—no matter how difficult or easy it may be—God is behind it and using that situation to make them better, stronger people who are ready to serve others in a real and lasting way.

> *Peggy says:*
> *Faith isn't just the ability to believe that*
> *God can change your circumstances;*
> *it's also the ability to believe that even if*
> *he leaves things the way they are, he will*
> *change you and give you the strength you*
> *need to endure whatever he allows to*
> *come your way.*
>
>

FAITH MEANS TALKING TO GOD
WHEN THINGS ARE TOUGH

Jeremy

My faith in God is a big part of me, and that's partly because I've grown up in a family where faith is practiced in very real ways in all kinds of life situations. My mom and dad are Christians. They may not be perfect in every way, but they always remember their faith in God when it's time to be grateful for something or when times get tough.

To me, having faith in God means that your life is different from other people's lives. You aren't better than they are, but you are different because God is living inside you.

My faith in God keeps me from doing some of the negative things so many kids do—drinking, drugs, and other things. My friends and I like to have fun and enjoy life, but we do it in ways we know show that we have faith in God and in ways that we know please him.

One of the ways my faith helps me is that it keeps me from worrying too much about what's in the future. Right now, I wouldn't change a thing about my life, and I give God the credit for all the good things he does for me and my family. One of the ways he has blessed us is by giving us our home, Roloff Farms. I've never known any other life than life on the farm, and I really don't want to know one yet. This is where I've grown up and where my family lives. It's where my friends come to hang out with me and where there are so many great memories.

But it wasn't all that long ago that it seemed like there was a chance we might have to sell the farm and move. The family was having money problems, and Dad and Mom talked about the possibility of losing the farm and having to live somewhere else. (They didn't tell us kids all the details, but when you live in the same house as someone, it's not that hard to figure out at least *some* of the things that are going on.)

If that had happened, I don't know what I would have done. But what I *did* do when that was all going on was the only thing I could: I prayed. I just prayed that God would somehow make a way for us to stay here in our home and that we wouldn't have to move. I knew then and I know now that God had a plan, and that he wasn't going to let us down and that he was going to take care of us no matter where we went. But I also know that I would have preferred—by a big margin—to stay where I was until I was ready to move out and start living my life as a grown-up.

I don't know everything there is to know about God and about the Bible, but I do know that God hears us when we pray, and when I had finished praying about our home, I felt a sense of peace as I left my bedroom and went downstairs. I just knew that no matter what, we were going to be OK.

I wouldn't say that that one prayer helped me to stop worrying completely. The worries and fears about what was happening to us came back sometimes. But when I was feeling bad or when I started worrying again, I prayed some more. I learned that one of the best things about prayer and about faith is that it helps you to trust God more to take care of the things you have no control over, and that however things work out, it was his decision and so has meaning.

Jeremy says:

Your faith in God is something you lean on even more when things aren't going well or when you are worried or scared that something might happen that you don't want to happen. When you have faith, you might find yourself worrying about things, but you can always take those worries to God because you know that he cares about you and has what is best for you in mind.

Roloff Family Value #9
Hard Work

Matt

IF I WERE TO tell you that I'm a total workaholic who spends most of his nonsleeping time at the office accomplishing things and making money, I'd be lying. Not only that, I wouldn't get away with it because Amy wouldn't let me!

But though I do like my sleep and like spending time enjoying myself with my family, I am a strong believer in a value called hard work. I am a person who believes in the productive use of his time and a person who believes that nearly all good things are accomplished through hard work and that little good can happen *without* hard work.

It has been said that luck is a combination of hard work meeting opportunity. And while I don't necessarily believe in luck, at least the way many people do, I do believe that nothing good can happen to you if you aren't willing to work hard and make the most of the opportunities that present themselves.

Amy and I were both brought up to value hard work, and it's still a part of who we are and a part of what we teach our children. We want them to understand that hard work, like so many of the values in this book, breeds more hard work and that laziness breeds more laziness.

I believe that hard work breeds creativity, innovation, and a raised level of satisfaction and feeling of accomplishment. And while hard work doesn't guarantee that everything you try will work out right, it does give you a sense of self-worth simply because even when you fail or don't accomplish all you set out to, at the end of the day you know that you gave what you were doing your all. On the other hand, those who receive something without having to work hard may enjoy what they have, but they won't have that sense of achievement.

One of my favorite sayings comes from one of the cofounders of the Hewlett-Packard Company, who once wrote, "Never put your tools away." That hit me as profound, because it suggests that I should be willing to work hard whenever the opportunity presents itself, and never stop.

So I put the value of hard work high on my list, and I can say that I am married to a woman who has done the same thing. Amy is one of the hardest-working mothers I've ever seen, and the results so far have been amazing.

Someone who has never been a stay-at-home mother has no idea how hard it is to raise children—especially four of them—and do it well. And while there are many things about Amy I appreciate and love, there is nothing I've admired more in her than her willingness to work hard to be the best mom she can be.

Amy

Aside from what we usually think of as "domestic" duties, raising children includes such things as disciplining them, talking with them, making sure they do their chores and their homework, reading, playing games, and loving them. And while that might not sound like work, it can be—and often is—emotionally taxing. It takes concentration to be a mother, because there are times when it would seem easy to just check out for a while. But you can't do that. You have to stick with it every day and do the things it takes to be a good mother.

We both believe it's our duty as parents to instill that work ethic into our children. We start by being an example to them of the value and the benefits of hard work. We make sure they work hard to excel in all they do—especially their studies and their homework.

We want our children to understand what we've learned in life: that working hard and applying yourself to being the best you can be in all you do may not produce instant benefits but will pay off in the long run. We want them to know that hard work isn't always fun but that if they want to achieve anything in life, they have to be willing to put in the time and the effort in whatever endeavor they choose. And that work will only make the achievement sweeter.

HARD WORK TO BUILD
OUR FUTURE

Matt

The hardest I ever worked in my life was the period just before and right after Amy and I were married. I was working for a computer company in California, and the amount of work I put in at that time was absolutely exhausting.

I remember working from the start of my regular day shift until five in the morning, looking out the window and watching the sun come up, and thinking, *All I want to do is lay my head down.* When I felt that I just couldn't go on, I would go take a nap for a few hours, then get up and get back at it.

I was able to work like that because I was motivated by my love for Amy and my desire to make a future for us. I worked ninety to a hundred hours a week so that I could build up my career, get myself out of debt, and build a nest egg for Amy and me. I was also inspired by the computer programs I was working on; I really enjoyed the work I was doing, and I did a lot of really good work.

While I don't necessarily recommend that a newly married person—or *any* married person, for that matter—

work those kinds of hours, I will say that doing so helped me build my career and make things easier for me as I got older. It helped build in me an appreciation for what hard work can do.

Today, I still value hard work, but more than that, I'm enjoying the benefits and rewards of all the hard work I put in all those years ago. One of those benefits was our farm. And while getting this farm in the shape it is in today also took a lot of work, it was something I enjoyed because it was a project for which I had passion.

There was an intense period of hard work involved in rebuilding and restoring the farm to the point where I could call it our home. We had to do excavation, carpentry, roofing, windows, cleanup—the list goes on . . . and on and on some more! In trying to get it all done, I felt like the Greek mythological character Sisyphus, the poor soul who was condemned for eternity to repeatedly rolling a boulder up to the peak of a mountain only to have it roll back down again. It seemed like there was a never-ending and ever-expanding list of things to do just to get the place livable.

I remember on several occasions working into the wee hours of the morning trying to get things done. I remember getting on my hands and knees and planting trees because I couldn't manage the big shovel any averaged-sized person would use to plant them. I remember getting so tired that I didn't know if I could go on, but at the same time feeling intensely motivated to get the place in shape so that I could stop. I remember hiring more and more laborers to help me get all the work done.

Eventually, I got to the point where I could sit back

and relax a little bit and enjoy the fruits of my labor. But as anyone who has ever lived on a farm knows, there is always hard work to be done. That's especially true of Roloff Farms because I had so many dreams and plans I wanted to fulfill before the kids were too old to enjoy them.

I've always wanted my children to understand that nothing they see around them—the house they live in and the farm they work and play on—could have happened if it weren't for hard work. I want them to understand that if they can dedicate themselves to making plans and working hard, they can accomplish anything they set out to do.

That is the attitude that was instilled in me many years ago, and it's one that has helped me make our farm what it has become. And it is one of the values I want to see instilled in my four kids.

Matt says:
If you want to accomplish anything important, if you want to see your dreams come true, you're going to have to work. Nothing good comes but through persistent, hard work.

HARD WORK HAS
ITS REWARDS

Amy

While our kids are growing up on a farm, the life of a farmer's son or farmer's daughter has changed over the past century. In the old days, a farmer's kids worked almost as hard as Dad did to plant and care for the crops, then harvest them and get them to the market.

Now things are different. While our four kids have spent every day of their lives living on Roloff Farms, they aren't extensions of Matt in that they are here to work. Now, their hard work (and it is that) is confined mostly to the homework their teachers assign. Yes, there is work to do on the farm, but Matt has a tendency—and I think it's a good one—to make even the hard work here look fun.

Matt is not physically able to do everything that needs to be done on our farm; he needs help. Sometimes that help comes from hired hands, but some of it comes from our kids, though sometimes it takes coaxing and cajoling—as well as a little bit of pay—to get them to do the things that need to be done around here.

That's what happened during our first pumpkin season here at Roloff Farms.

The boys—mostly Zachary—had done a great job planting the pumpkin plants in the spring, and after that the pumpkins did the rest. Come September and October, we could see we were going to have a bumper crop of pumpkins at Roloff Farms.

When it came time for harvest, Matt and I told the kids—especially Zachary and Jeremy, because of their age and ability to do the things that needed to be done—that we needed them to be available to help out with showing people around the farm, with harvesting the pumpkins, moving them, and with other tasks.

At first, the boys complained and grumbled a little bit, telling Matt and me that they had other things to do. But when we let them know how much we needed them in order to make the pumpkin harvest a success, they were willing to step up and help out in any way they could. Zachary did a great job driving the tractor and taking people on tours of the farm, and Jeremy did a great job of interacting with the people and taking them on walking tours around other parts of our farm. It wasn't hard physical labor, but it did take up a lot of their time and energy for four weekends in a row.

Matt and I grew up in a time and in a culture where hard work was valued, where people spent the days of their youth establishing a work ethic and getting started doing the things it took for their families to prosper. And while the value and meaning of hard work has changed since then, it's still important in the Roloff family that our kids understand how valuable hard work is—both for present benefits and for those in the future.

Amy says:
Hard work doesn't always mean physical,
backbreaking labor. Sometimes it means
sacrificing your time to do what your family
needs done when you'd rather be doing
something else.

WORKING HARD TILL
THE JOB IS DONE

Zachary

One of the things Dad and Mom teach me as the only little person among their four children is that in order to accomplish something, I will probably have to work longer and harder than average-height people who are doing the same work I do.

No one says that's fair—I don't think it is—but that's the way life is for a little person. We are automatically seen as being at a disadvantage in nearly everything we do, and we have to work hard to overcome both people's perceptions and our own physical limitations.

Late in October, more visitors come to our farm to buy pumpkins and tour the farm than we can welcome. Last year alone, more than thirty thousand people came!

Not many people really think about how the pumpkins got there in the first place, but I'll tell you anyway: for the most part, I was the one who planted them.

Dad had bought some pumpkin seeds and got the plants started in a greenhouse, and once they were ready to be put in the ground outside, he hired me, Jeremy, and some of our friends to do the planting. After negotiating our pay with Dad, we set out to get the job done. Dad left for a business trip, fully expecting the pumpkins to be planted by the time he got home.

The conditions that day were perfect for all of us to make short work of planting the pumpkin seedlings. It was a little cloudy and the temperature was just right. We got started on the planting, but it wasn't long before we realized that it was going to be hard work getting them all in the ground—so hard, in fact, that Jeremy and his friends quit and left me alone to do all the work.

Working together, it wouldn't have taken all of us long to finish the project, but with most of the plants still waiting to be put in the ground, I was alone. I didn't want to disappoint Dad, and I knew he wasn't going to be happy if we didn't get that project finished. I also knew that when he got home, he would send us back out to get it done anyway. Besides, I still wanted to get paid. So instead of quitting like the other guys had, I got busy planting.

It took me about two hours to finish planting the pumpkins. It was pretty hard work, and I had to do a lot of bending and stretching to get it done. But still I thought to myself that my brother and my friends should have been able to tough it out and finish the job with me. If I could do it, then they should be able to also!

When I finished planting the pumpkin patch, I felt sore and tired, but I also felt a sense of accomplishment because I had finished something I started. I was also proud of myself because I didn't quit and because I did it all by myself.

As it was, Dad gave me a pat on the back and a "Good

job, Zach!" But there was one other thing. He paid me what he said he would for the work, and he gave me a little bonus too.

That's what you get when you stick with a project and work hard to get it finished. You get the pay you were told you'd get—and maybe something extra!

> *Zachary says:*
> *Working hard is good for you because people will want to hire you knowing you'll get the job finished and finished the right way.*

Roloff Family Value #10
Integrity

Matt

PARENTS JUST CAN'T BE the kind of parents they need to be for their children unless they take the time to instill in their kids the personal value known as integrity. We don't claim to be perfect in our integrity, but what we do claim is to understand how important it is to know right from wrong and to act on what you know.

There are a lot of definitions of integrity. Some people say integrity means letting your yes be yes and your no be no—in other words, keeping your word no matter what. Others think integrity means being honest about everything, no matter the cost. Still others would say it's the quality of doing what you know is right, even when doing something else might benefit you for the moment. Integrity could also be defined as choosing to do the right thing when you think no one is watching, simply because it's right and because you know that no matter how far away from others you might feel in a given moment, God is watching.

Those are all great definitions of the word *integrity*, and I wouldn't offer so much as a small argument against any of them, but if I were to define that word, I'd say that it's the quality of always being true to who you are, in all circumstances and in all situations.

For the Roloff family, integrity means living by the values we've been discussing, the ones that make us the family we've become. And it's integrity that helps us to stick to these values.

There are some values that are beyond simple differences in focus. They are, to us, issues of integrity. They include faith, love for one another, and hard work. Those are the things you focus on and act on simply because it's the right thing to do. Not focusing on them and acting on them would mean we lacked integrity.

Having integrity doesn't mean you are perfect. But it means that you do what is right—at least to the best of your ability—in all areas of your life.

Integrity is also essential in personal relationships. When you have this kind of integrity, you know how to treat people the way you want to be treated yourself—also known as living by the Golden Rule, doing to others what you'd have them do to you.

That means being fair with them in all matters, keeping your word to them no matter how much it may inconvenience you, and being loyal to them in whatever way is appropriate to the relationship. That goes for our business relationships, for our personal relationships (friendships, romances, and so forth), and our relationships within the family.

When it comes to integrity in our personal relationships, we try teach the kids—through both our words and actions—to understand how important it is that they treat others fairly and justly, all the while holding to what they know is right and avoiding what is wrong.

An important part of integrity is the ability to recognize that you've done something wrong or something that hurt another person, confess that wrongdoing to that person, and do whatever it takes to make amends. We don't want our children to ever believe they can just "get away" with doing something wrong or with hurting another person—even if there are no tangible consequences. We want them to understand the importance of doing right by all people, no matter what kind of relationship they have with them.

We do our best to instill these things in our children on a day-to-day basis. It isn't always easy or comfortable or convenient—as you will see in some of the following examples—but it's part of who we are as a family and as individuals.

We want our children to know that when they have integrity, people will know that they can count on them to do, be, and say what they truly are, and to do what is right.

TEACHING INTEGRITY
ISN'T ALWAYS EASY

Amy

I don't think there's an adult around today who doesn't recall a childhood incident in which they learned the importance of integrity and honesty. I know I remember a few, and so does Matt. In many ways, learning those things—as difficult as the lessons may be—is a rite of passage for a child.

I remember well how it was for one of my own.

I was out grocery shopping with my youngest son, Jacob, who was in first or second grade at the time. As we passed the candy rack, so strategically placed next to the checkout stand, Jacob saw something he wanted. As I was unloading the groceries from my cart, Jacob tapped me on the shoulder and asked, "Mom, can we buy this?"

There have been times when I've allowed the kids to pick up something at the checkout stand, but not this time. "Jacob, you can't ask for something each and every time we go grocery shopping," I told him. "You can have something when we get home."

I didn't give it another thought until we were back at the car loading up our groceries. As I finished, I looked at Jacob and noticed that he had something in his pocket that wasn't there when we went into the store. I knew it wasn't anything I had bought.

"What is this, Jacob?" I asked him.

"Well, I got this at the store," he said innocently.

"What do you mean you got it at the store?" I asked him. "I know I didn't buy it. So did you just take it?"

Jacob looked at me with those big brown eyes and long eyelashes, and I knew what had happened. I knew he had taken something he shouldn't have and that I had to take him back to the store and teach him a lesson in honesty and integrity.

"Come on, Jacob," I said. "We have to go back."

I could just as easily have gone back into the store, explained what had happened as a mistake, and paid for what my son had taken. But I knew this had to be a learning time for him. He was really scared as I took him back in the store to talk to the manager. It broke my heart as a parent to see my son's eyes well up with tears, but at the same time I wanted him to understand that you can't just take something you want without paying for it. Not only that, I wanted him to understand that when you make a mistake like that, you have to own up to it and make amends.

I went into the store and spoke to the manager and explained what had happened, then asked him to come and talk to Jacob. "What do you need to tell the man, Jacob?" I asked, then waited for him to confess what he had done. After a few moments of silence, Jacob told the manager, "I took some gum. I'm sorry I did that."

The manager, speaking in a firm but gentle voice, asked Jacob, "Do you realize that what you did is wrong?

Do you realize that this is serious stuff and you could get in big trouble and that it's not right to take things from other people?"

By this time, Jacob was in tears. "I know!" he sobbed. "I'm sorry I did that!"

Although I didn't enjoy seeing my son so upset, I knew that it was necessary for him to learn the importance of honesty and integrity and of protecting his reputation. He needed to understand that if he takes things that don't belong to him, people won't trust him, and they'll suspect him if something he didn't take comes up missing. I wanted him to know that you never really get away with doing wrong, even if you don't pay the consequences right away.

> *Amy says:*
> *It is sometimes difficult to teach children*
> *the importance of honesty and integrity.*
> *But remember, it's one of the most*
> *important lessons they can ever learn.*
>
>

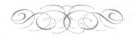

BEING AN EXAMPLE
OF INTEGRITY

Matt

One of the reasons I value integrity is that I know that my children are watching what I do to see if what I say I believe matches up with the things I do. There have been several incidents with my kids when I had a chance to demonstrate what integrity means.

During the pumpkin season there were some severe traffic flow problems in the area one weekend. What's worse is that a lot of the people who came ended up parking their cars in my neighbors' fields. Nothing was damaged and no crops or livestock were lost, and for the most part my neighbors were good about it. But I still felt that I should compensate them for their trouble.

Call it aggravation pay if you want, but I couldn't just allow them to be troubled without their getting something out of it. For one thing, it was a matter of integrity. For another, it was a matter of being a good neighbor! I didn't feel that an apology was going to cut it, so I had our bookkeeper cut my neighbors checks in amounts I felt compensated them fairly.

I was glad that I could demonstrate to my neighbors

some neighborliness and some integrity in dealing with what we'd put them through—even if we hadn't meant it to turn out that way. But more than that, I'm happy that my children saw that I am someone who wants to do right by people, even when the trouble I've caused them wasn't intentional.

I can't honestly claim that I've always done the right thing or that I have always been perfect in my integrity. There have been plenty of times in my life when I haven't done what I would do today if I were faced with the same situation. I've regretted the things I've done, and when it was possible, I've tried to go back and make amends.

I've been thinking lately that it would be good if I had more opportunities to demonstrate to my children what integrity means and how important it is to have it in all their relationships. I hope and pray for some small situations where a cashier at the local supermarket gives me change for a twenty-dollar bill when I had tendered a ten. Or where the ticket person at the theater tries to sell me a child's ticket for my overage son or daughter.

When and if something like that happens, I will use it to my advantage and my children's advantage to show them that it's far better to do what is right than to save five or ten dollars. I will make sure I do what is right and fair, and I'll pay what needs to be paid.

That will be the best five or ten dollars I could ever spend!

> *Matt says:*
> *Integrity is something a mother and*
> *father should always strive not just to*
> *teach but also to demonstrate in real-life*
> *situations to their children in any and*
> *every way possible.*

BEING TRUE TO YOURSELF

Zachary

As members of the Little People of America, we Roloffs always look forward to the yearly convention. It's a time when we can get together with friends we may see only once a year and a time when we can meet and greet LPs from all over the nation.

One of the things you'd see if you were to go to an LPA convention is that little people can party just as hard as the average-sized. And from everything I've seen, it's easy for underage people to get all the alcohol they want and to get into the other kinds of trouble my family has taught me to stay out of. I don't want to make it sound like the people who go to the convention go there just so they can get out of control once a year. For the most part, the people who go there have a good time but do it within limits. But there is partying like there would be if it were a gathering of any other group.

I watch what goes on at the conventions, and it looks to me like the people who run them—the hotel staff, the bartenders, and the waitpeople—don't always pay close attention to the ages of the people they are serving.

One of the things Mom always talks to me about before we go to the LPA convention is the need for me to be careful about what kind of activities I get into. I have never wanted to get into drinking or drug use or anything like that, but Mom still talks to me and reminds me that I have to be true to myself and avoid those things.

Mom does that because she knows that anyone can be tempted or even tricked into doing things he or she knows aren't right. She also knows kids want to do what other kids are doing, things they wouldn't otherwise do. Mom knows that I'm pretty strong when it comes to avoiding those kinds of things, but she still wants to make sure that I'm aware of the temptations in these settings so I can avoid them.

I appreciate how my mom takes the time to talk to me and my brothers and sister about those things, and I'm glad that she reminds us to have the integrity to do what we know is right even when we see others doing wrong, and to be strong enough in our characters to say no to it and not take advantage of the lack of supervision.

> *Zachary says:*
> *Integrity means doing the things you know are right and avoiding the things you know are wrong, even when you can "get away with it."*
>
>

Roloff Family Value #11
Dreaming Dreams
and Making Plans

Matt

I BELIEVE IT'S SAFE to say that no one has ever accomplished anything noteworthy without first daring to dream about it. No great invention or idea started without someone's developing a dream, then acting on it.

All the great developments in human history—the

lightbulb, the telephone, the television, the Internet, and the automobile, just to name a few—started with someone who had a dream about meeting what they believed was a real human need. Thomas Edison, Alexander Graham Bell, and Henry Ford didn't all just wake up one morning and decide to throw together inventions that would revolutionize human life. Theirs were inventions that took years of dreaming and planning.

When you spend weeks on end lying in bed—in a hospital or at home—recovering from major surgery, as I did, you have a lot of time to think. That is how I learned how to dream. For example, I can remember as I lay in bed, sometimes barely able to move, dreaming about how I wanted to build the best go-cart around. I would think for hours on end about the design, about how it would look, and how I could make it go by using the strong Bay Area wind.

Eventually, that dream became a plan, and from there it became a reality. And not only did I get to build a great go-cart, I learned early the value both of being a dreamer and a visionary and of setting high goals.

This is one area in which Amy and I are different. While she has respect for my ability to dream and the importance of setting goals, she is a more practical person. She recognizes the importance of setting goals, and she encourages me and the kids to do just that, but my approach is that you can't accomplish anything without first setting goals, and you can't set worthy goals without first daring to dream.

Having a dream and setting a goal-go hand-in-hand,

just like love and marriage in the old Frank Sinatra song. As Ol' Blue Eyes sang, you really can't have one without the other. That's why the ability to dream and the daring to pursue the dream are a big part of what makes the Roloff home what it is today.

However, I do recognize that there is a difference between the two. A dream is an idea or a vision of something you would like to do "one day when . . ." Setting a goal means putting a plan with that dream. Goals should be achievable with the resources you have or will have at hand. I believe in setting goals that stretch me, but I also believe in being practical.

One of the biggest mistakes people make when it comes to goal setting is that they set unrealistic goals. For example, I always knew better than to set a goal of playing professional football, baseball, or basketball. I understood at a very young age that the body God gave me, as grateful as I am for it, would never be suited for professional sports. For me, setting goals for any physical activity was going to have to start with just being able to get around well enough to function in the world I live in.

When I talk about daring to dream, I'm not talking about wasting time indulging in idle daydreams or unattainable fantasies. I'm talking specifically about developing a plan or a desire for which you have a real passion. I'm talking about having a vivid mental picture of something you want to do in life, something that is at the same time visionary and realistic.

I love daring people to dream and to set high goals, and that includes my wife and children. I love challenging them to set their sights above where they are and to dream of accomplishing more than they've accomplished—maybe even more than they'd ever considered or dreamed of accomplishing. And I hope they can look at me and some of the dreams I had that became a reality and be inspired to do the same in their lives.

DEALING WITH MY HUSBAND'S DREAMS AND PLANS

Amy

I'll admit, I'm not much of a dreamer. However, that doesn't keep me from respecting Matt's creativity and his ability to dream and act on those dreams. I value those things because I know how hard it is to find them together in one man. And while I am more of a planner than Matt is, I still love the fact that he's an idea guy and that he's not afraid to tell me when he's got an idea or dream brewing in his head, no matter how big or small.

And even though I give Matt grief about the projects he dreams up and plans for and starts around the house and the farm, I am his biggest supporter when he pulls something off and makes it work. I absolutely love it when his dreams become visions, his visions become plans, and his plans become reality!

One of Matt's recent plans is the zip line he put up on the farm. A zip line is a steel cable that runs from one spot to another high off the ground with a set of pulleys that allow people to hang on it and ride from one place to another. The genesis of Matt's dream of having one on the farm was a trip we took to Hawaii, where Matt and the kids all had a great time riding a zip line.

Being one not to just copy what he's seen elsewhere but instead to take things up a notch, Matt wanted to build a zip line on the farm that was bigger, faster, and higher than the one in Hawaii. And it wasn't long before he put some actual planning behind his idea.

I have to admit that my first reaction when Matt brought up the idea of the zip line was "Why do we need it?" That's part of my personality. I like dreams as much as the next person, but I am more prone than Matt to ask questions such as "Why?" "How?" and "How much will it cost?" In the case of the zip line, I also wondered who would ride it and whether it was a dangerous risk to have one on our property.

And then there was my other question, which is why Matt wants to do this project when there are so many things we could use in the house. Instead of the zip line, how about the molding and trim inside the house? What about that garage we've been talking about for so long so that we don't have to leave our cars out in the rain? Yes, I like the fun projects, but I tend to focus on the more practical things we need to do.

But Matt was not to be deferred, and within the year, his vision became a reality. He had done all the planning and acquired the help he needed to create the zip line, which to this day stretches 860 feet, just slightly longer than the one they rode in Hawaii. The kids love it!

Despite my own misgivings, I had said from the beginning that it would be great if this project works, and it certainly has. It's exciting to me to see Matt's dreams become a reality, especially when they are for the benefit of our children.

> *Amy says:*
> One of the great things a parent can do for a child is show him how to dream and turn those dreams into reality—even when those dreams don't at first seem to make perfect sense to everyone else.
>
>

SEEING PAST WHAT *IS* TO
WHAT *COULD BE*

Matt

Our farm has become quite a spectacle and, at certain times of the year, quite an attraction.

But the farm hasn't always looked the way it does today. In fact, when we bought it back in 1990, it was a broken down wreck of a property with a beat-up, rundown house, an overgrown peach orchard, a barn that would have fit in on the old TV show *Green Acres*, and a bunch of old junker cars sitting around.

When I first saw that farm in Oregon, I was twenty-eight years old and had just quit a great job designing software in Silicon Valley in California. Amy was six months pregnant with our twins, Jeremy and Zachary, and we'd just bought a beautiful new home in California.

But to call the house on the farm we were looking at a dump is an insult to some of the dumps I've seen. It was literally filled with trash. The roof, what there was of it, leaked like a sieve, and the paint was peeling off the house's worn-out siding.

There was nothing about the place to really draw the

eye, other than the fact that it was set among some very pretty and potentially productive farmland. It was thirty-four acres of anything you could imagine set at the end of a quarter-mile-long gravel road.

But the moment I first saw the place, I began dreaming about what it could be. The first thing I thought was how great it would be for Amy and me to raise our children in a place like this. There were trees to climb, a barn to play in, and acreage enough for them to run in all day long if they wanted to.

I began dreaming about turning this piece of property into not just productive farmland (it now produces some of the finest peaches in northwest Oregon) but also a place where my children could enjoy some of the things that I missed out on as a child.

I began dreaming about a place that would be *fun* for me, Amy, and my children to call home. Those dreams grew too. I bought the property soon after I'd first seen it, and it wasn't long before it started to take shape. It didn't happen overnight, and it didn't happen without us putting a lot of work, a lot of time, and a lot of money into it. But happen it did, and today it is a home that truly qualifies as unique.

If you were to look at the farm now and then look at the pictures of it when we first bought it, you might have a hard time believing that it's the same place. The house has been completely rebuilt and remodeled; it has a traditional farmhouse look—complete with front porch and surrounding deck—with some special modifications for the three little people who live there.

Over the years I have made far more changes to the farm than I can list here, and there are also more dreams in my head and plans on the drawing board. And all these things have happened and are happening because we are a family that values the ability to dream dreams and make plans to make those dreams a reality.

Matt says:
One of the great things about dreaming dreams and making plans is that you learn to see beyond what something is right now to what it has the potential to be in the future. And each success (or failure) helps you reach for the next dream more easily.

A PLAN THAT
BECAME REALITY

Zachary

I think Mom and Dad have passed something on to me when it comes to dreaming dreams and making plans. Dad is the one who dreams, and Mom is the one who plans, and between the two of them, I've learned how to do some of both.

My dreams are probably more realistic than Dad's, and I'm probably more likely to take the time to plan something out to make sure it happens. A good example of that was in the Dwarf Athletic Association of America (DAAA) Twentieth Anniversary games in 2006. The DAAA games are held every year in conjunction with the Little People of America convention. In 2006, the games and the convention were held in Milwaukee, Wisconsin. There was competition in basketball, track and field, swimming, volleyball, weight lifting, soccer, and some other events.

Since soccer is and always has been my game, I wanted to put together a team for the games. I wanted to get together a group of people who would have a good chance of winning the tournament, and I especially wanted to have a good chance at beating the Los Angeles Breakers, a group of little people who have made their name playing some pretty good basketball. For the most part, it's fun and friendly competition, but I knew I wanted to beat them bad.

The first step in getting the team together was making a lot of phone calls to people I thought would be interested in playing—and who could play well enough to compete at the DAAA games. I called people I knew from all over the country trying to get together enough people for the team. After some effort, we had a group of guys and gals (it was a coed competition) who made up our team, which we called the Grasshogs.

The plan was to play the Breakers in both soccer and basketball. I had my focus on beating them in soccer, because that's the game I love and the game I'm better at. I also knew that beating them in basketball probably wasn't realistic because they were one of the best little people basketball teams around, having won several national championships and some world championships too.

Basketball was first, and the Breakers beat us *bad*, going on to win the tournament. I had hoped we would do better against them in basketball, but my real goal was taking first place in that soccer tournament. And beating the Breakers.

The Breakers' players told everybody that they would win 3-1. I knew we could play better defense than that! We did, too. In fact, we held the Breakers without a goal for the whole first half, then scored a goal just before halftime, and we were able to hold them off through the second half to win 1-0. Goal met! It felt great.

The whole thing showed me how important it was that I took the time to set a goal and make a plan for the soccer tournament. I'd had to contact everyone, buy the jerseys and T-shirts, create a logo, and make sure people showed up and registered to play. It had all seemed very daunting at first, maybe a goal that was too hard to reach, but when I took it step by step, each step seemed to bring me closer to my goal.

Zachary says:
When the goal seems big and the plan looks tough, just start and soon the next thing you need to do will look possible. Step by step you can get through anything.

A SMALL MAN
WITH BIG DREAMS

Ron

When Matt was growing up, he had a lot of big dreams, and some of them involved participating in sports that his mother and I thought he had no business thinking about. Matt dreamed of being a great basketball player, a great skier, a great wrestler, a great bicycle rider—the list goes on and on.

It comes as a surprise to a lot of people to find out that sports and athletics are a big part of a lot of little people's lives. Matt is a great example. Matt took part in a lot of athletic competitions over the years. He competed in several sports activities for physically challenged students, and he was even able to compete successfully in high school wrestling.

He used to tell us that he could do those things because he had "done it in my mind." He meant that if he could visualize himself doing something, then he felt he would actually be able to do it if he worked toward that goal he imagined. That focus helped allow Matt to have a decent wrestling career in high school. Matt admits that he wasn't a great wrestler, but he had a winning record and even won the district tournament a few times wrestling at the ninety-five-pound weight division.

I guess that is part of being a dreamer—and Matt is

certainly that—and part of what has allowed him to do things many who know him said he shouldn't be doing. Peg and I had our misgivings about a lot of the things Matt wanted to do, but we bit our lips, said our prayers, and allowed him to do things some parents in our position wouldn't have allowed their son to do.

One great example was Matt's dream of becoming a skier. He first became hooked on skiing in junior high school when we went on a family ski trip. Matt was quite the hot dog on the ski slopes, and he was as fearless on his skis as anyone—tall or short. He would take on the steepest slopes and fly down them at breakneck speeds, going over moguls and going airborne along the way. It was amazing to see the things he did on skis. It would have been amazing to see anyone do what he did, but it was all the more so because this was a young man with some serious physical limitations, a young man who had been through several extensive surgeries just so he could walk with the aid of crutches.

Matt went on from his first experience skiing to compete in several events for physically challenged people. We were always proud of him for being able to compete successfully on the slopes. But I was never more proud—I was even in awe—of what he did than one day when he took me skiing at one of his favorite spots at Lake Tahoe.

Matt took me up one of the most extreme runs in that whole resort, a run he told me was called a "black diamond." As we went up the lift, he was excited. He just couldn't wait to share with Dad something he was so passionate about. He was just sure that I was going to enjoy this run as much as he did.

As we got to the end of the ride on the lift and then

moved over to the top of the run, I looked down—and I mean almost *straight* down—at what I'd allowed my son to get me into. It was almost like looking directly over the ledge of a tall building. I knew there was no way I was going to make this run—at least not the way Matt was.

At that point, all I could think was *I want to live!*

"C'mon, Dad!" Matt cried out as he took off down the hill. I saw him crisscrossing, doing jumps and twists, and, in my mind anyway, paying no regard to life and limb. I, on the other hand, knew I wouldn't survive this run unless I kept my ski tips together and cut back and forth down the hill.

What I saw in Matt that day is the same sense of adventure and courage, the same ability to dream of something big and then do it, that he instills in his children to this day. That ability is part of what makes the Roloff family something special to this day.

> *Ron says:*
> *Part of being able to dream and plan*
> *is being willing to try to do the things—*
> *sometimes at the edge of your abilities—*
> *that others might not think you can.*
> *When you do that, what you accomplish*
> *can surprise those close to you . . .*
> *and maybe even yourself.*
>
>

Acknowledgments

A wonderful feeling came over us on the way to getting this project published: We started to reflect on how many people we are grateful to for the positive influences they've had in our lives and for helping instill in us an overcoming attitude.

Thanks to our families—parents Ron and Peg, Gordon and Pat, and our siblings—for helping to make our lives the joy and experience it has been.

Thanks to our amazing and unique children, Jeremy, Zachary, Molly, and Jacob—you are truly God's greatest earthly blessings to us. You not only bring us joy and happiness, but you are also an instrument used daily by God to make us not just better parents but better people too.

Thanks to our many friends who have always shown us love, supported us, given us advice, and encouraged us to keep reaching beyond life's minimums: There are many of you. Thanks also to those people who have made a difference in my life in so many ways: to all the people who helped me build my farm and reality out of my visions and dreams.

I'd like to thank the American people for their understanding of and accommodations for little people and others with disabilities. Thanks to the United States Congress for the Americans with Disabilities Act.

Special thanks to the people at Simon & Schuster for their patience and guidance in making this project happen. Thanks to Tracy Sumner for his patience in interviewing us and putting on paper what our family values really are, and also to Richard Mann for his editing support in getting this book completed.

Lastly and most important, thanks to the Lord Jesus Christ, who gives us life and who enabled me to see past my disability to become all that I could.

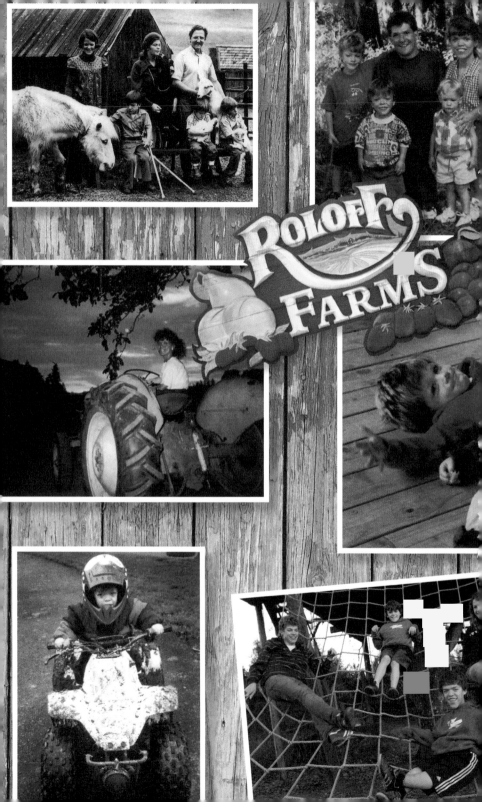